THE
MUTUAL RELATIONS
OF THE
FOUR CASTES
ACCORDING TO THE
MANAVADHARMAÇASTRAM.

Owing to the antiquity and rarity of this book, certain pages are regrettably absent, and readability is compromised due to the blurring of the original text. If you possess any insights regarding the availability of these missing sections, kindly inform us. Your assistance is crucial in ensuring the completion of this significant work for the benefit of future generations.

THE MUTUAL RELATIONS OF THE FOUR CASTES ACCORDING TO THE MANAVADHARMAÇASTRAM.

BY

EDWARD W. HOPKINS

GYAN

Published by

Gyan Publishing House
5, Ansari Road
Daryaganj, New Delhi-110002
Phone: 011-47034999, 9811692060
E-mail: books@gyanbooks.com

Distribution Network
gyanbooks.com
India, USA, Canada, UK, Australia

ISBN: 978-93-6208-606-8 (HB)
First Published, 1881

2nd Impression 2024

Printed at: Gyan Press, Delhi.

THE MUTUAL RELATIONS OF THE FOUR CASTES ACCORDING TO THE MANAVADHARMAÇASTRAM

Author: EDWARD W. HOPKINS

THE
MUTUAL RELATIONS
OF THE
FOUR CASTES
ACCORDING TO THE
MĀNAVADHARMAÇĀSTRAM.

BY

EDWARD W. HOPKINS, PH. DR.

LEIPZIG
BREITKOPF AND HÄRTEL.
1881.

PREFACE.

In undertaking to collate, even upon a small and limited field, the dicta of a text whose original form is as yet by no means certain, I am not unaware of the criticisms which might be brought against such a proceeding, nor am I wholly able to forestall them. It is doubtless true that the more we examine those Dharmaçāstra, the date of which we can place with surety at a period subsequent to that of the manavic text, the more cautiously we must answer the question, what part of our work is of later origin, and what part we may permit to remain as a genuine portion of the Mān.dh.çās. We can say, for instance, with tolerable assurance that M. VIII 168 does not belong to the work as it originally stood; yet, if we based this statement upon the fact that the çloka occurs again in the dh.çās. of Nārada (IV 55) (v. Jolly, Ueber das Indische Schuldrecht S. 290) we should certainly be too hasty in our judgement, for, unless we have grounds other than the mere outward agreement, we have no right to the assumption that the çloka is to be rejected from the earlier text. In this particular case «balād yaccāpi lekhitam» is convincing proof, for writing is not elsewhere recognized by Manu. Without such grounds, however, we can not say that a çloka like this is not, instead of being interpolated in the earlier, simply copied from this into the later text.

In spite of this uncertainty, however, which only careful criticism of each such care can clear away, the Mān.dh.çās. offers us, all in all, without doubt the earliest complete form of the dh.çās. literature. It is a work which has been regarded as the original authority in the law, and though with the dh. sūtra before us we can no longer claim for it the high antiquity which early scholars assigned to it, nor even a special and peculiar origin, yet it still remains that great body of the law which shows us the first completed development of legal science, and as such it must always stand at the head of the Indian law-literature. Whatever later researches shall have to object against particular passages, we yet have, in general, the chief work of its kind that Indian genius has produced — a work which forms in itself a completed and elaborated whole — and in this light special investigations confined to the manavic text may perhaps not be unfruitful.

If we turn from the text critique to the history of the dh.çās. we find more satisfactory results. Sanskṛt scholarship has done away with the flighty account of the origin of this work given us by the credulous Hindu. Not only Manu as creator of the world and revealer of the dh.çās., but Manu as a personal law-giver — in the sense that he composed independently the so-called law-book which bears his name — has vanished. We know that the work was the result of a gradual development (as in the case of other Indian law-books) from more primitive beginnings. We can moreover assign it its proper position in relation to other Sk. literature. It is a legitimate growth from the attempts at law-making as promulgated by the school of the Black Yajur Veda. Cf. Weber, Ind. Lit.-Geschichte (2. Auflage) S. 295,6. M. Müller, Hist. Anc. Sk. Lit. p. 134. Johäntgen, Ueber das Gesetzbuch des Manu, S. 100. In the digest of Hindu Law of Inheritance (West and Bühler, 2nd Ed. 1878) the opinion is plainly spoken that the dh.çās. of Manu and Yājñavalkya are versifications of older sūtra. This sūtram of Manu is preliminary to the çāstram, as most prose sūtra are prior to poetic çāstra. Weber's keenness had long prophecied a gṛhyasūtram as inferable from the fact that most dh.çās. pre-suppose a gṛhyasūtram. This text has been found, and is now, though in a corrupt state, being edited. According to Schroeder (Gesammt-Sitzung vom 24. Juli 1879 [Berlin]) the origin of the work can be still more precisely settled. To quote his own words (S. 701): «Es liegt nicht der mindeste grund vor, das Mānavadharmaçāstram von den zu Māitrāyaṇīçākhā gehörigen Mānava-werken zu trennen».

We know then that the law-book of Manu belongs to the school of the Black Yajuḥ, and more particularly to that branch known as the Māitrāyaṇī, one of the numerous divisions of this Veda, of which the Mānava works are in general a subdivision. The authorship of the text, as Johäntgen and Schroeder agree, was not claimed by the school in which it originated, in order that their law-book might attain the more power by being ascribed to an aboriginal Manu. In this sense alone can we speak of Manu and Manu's law-book.

With respect to this essay, the first paragraphs explain sufficiently the object of the work. As to the arrangement, I trust the somewhat illogical deferring of the mutual Br. Ksh. relations till the end of the discussion, thus coming after Vaiç. and Çūd., will be considered justified by the fact that these are the parties about which the principal questions cluster. I had originally affixed to the little work four appendices, which I have at present, from sundry reasons, refrained from printing, and I can here only indicate their contents, which has in some degree affected the dissertation. The first, in regard to Vadha, is an attempt to trace the growth of significance which this term experienced; it being, as I think, not an expression of entirely ambiguous meaning in the dh.çās., as maintained by P. W., but one the development of whose meaning we can trace in our present law-books. The second appendix, regarding the mixed castes or classes, might perhaps have been looked for in the essay itself. I have preferred, however, to confine myself to the four pure castes. The great majority of statements respecting *varṇasaṃkara* is given together with some attempt at systemization in the tenth book. Under the third appendix, «women in reference to caste», I have grouped some citations which might also have been expected in the main work. The omission of these quotations I can only rectify by citing here those çl. which treat in some way of the different castes — though none of them are of much importance, being all relative to women: Intercourse of dvijas with low women III 19. XI 179. XI 176; marriage III 20 to 44, 12 to 17; seduction by different castes VIII 364 flg., and 374 flg. (with the great inconsequentness contained in this passage); penalty for slaughter of women according to caste XI 139; property of sons of a Br. IX 150 flg., and IX 122 flg.; Çūd.'s çulkam IX 98. to 100, III 51. The last, unended, appendix, a review of the earlier literature unentioned by Manu with a tabular synopsis of the parallel çlokas between Mān.dh.çās. and other law-books, I would gladly have appended here; the second part, however, advances too slowly to completion. I have refrained in the text from giving any parallel passages, except occasionally to the dh. sūtra and (more frequently) to Yāj., as I desired the investigation to be as much as possible only in respect to the Mān.dh.çās. These, together with the chance quotations from Mbhā., are chiefly for the purpose of illustrating and explaining the manavic text, but no thorough comparison has been attempted.

The edition from which I quote is that of Vidyāsāgara (Calc. 1874), which agrees in numbering with that of Loiseleur except in admitting in book eleven the çloka following no. 51. In Jones and Loiseleur this is rejected. References after çl. 52 are therefore one in advance of L.'s text. The çl. is not in Jones's text but stands in the translation. Quotations from J. are according to Haughton's Edition (1825). References are made to the Calcutta edition rather than to L.'s on account of the commentary.

In the transcription of the Sk. I have followed the plan recommended by Whitney, in the Proceed. Am. Or. Soc. Oct. 1880, as regards the macron and ṛ-vowel, retaining, however, sh for the lingual sibilant, since, as it seems to me, though less consequent than ṣ, it is practically much easier to write.

Leipzig in Jan. 1881.

The object of this essay is to attempt a systematic presentation of the mutual relations of the four castes of Indian society as they are found in the so called Law-book of Manu, together with the discussion of such side questions as may seem to have important bearing on the results to be obtained from the investigation.

We have two works of importance in regard to the relations of Hindu castes: Weber «Collectanea über die Kastenverhältnisse in den Brāhmaṇa und Sūtra» Indische Studien, Bd. X, and Muir «Original Sanskṛt Texts» Vol. I. The latter of these treats of the «mythical and legendary accounts of the origin of caste with an inquiry into its existence in the vedic age», the former of the notices of caste relations found in the literature of the Brhm. and Sûtra.[1] Muir touches upon the relations of castes in Manu only where the latter presents such points as are indicated by the supplementary title of the Or. Sk. Texts, and Weber's quotations since they are principally from Gobhila, Kauç., Pärask., Çat. Brm., Tait. Saṃh. and so forth scarcely do more than notice here and there an agreement with the manavic law-book or touch upon an incongruity in that work. What this valuable contribution of Weber's

1) The one careful and (by Weber) justly praised monograph on Manu (Johäntgen, Über das Gesetzbuch des Manu) deals with the philosophical theories advanced in the law-book. The author shows that the germ of Buddhistic philosophy is to be sought for in our text and the development of this teaching in that of Yäjñavalkya — in the one the sāṃkhya of Kapila and in the other the yoga of Patañjali. —

has done for this literature I hope in part to complement by an exhibition of these relations on the narrow province of the Mānavà Dharmaçāstram. This work is generally supposed to present the completion of the caste system and to show us the state of Indian society at a time when the Brahm. caste had reached the apex of its power and the fetters of caste had been clamped with the last rivet of a gradually wide spread, deep rooted superstition, propagated by an unscrupulous and overweening priestly aristocracy.

Prof. Weber himself speaks as follows on this subject: (Indische Literatur-Geschichte S. 294) Diese letztere (die Brâhmanische Staatsordnung) tritt uns denn auch in der That in dem ältesten dieser Werke, dem Gesetzbuche des Manu, in ganzer Vollendung entgegen. Der Br. hat das Ziel, welchem er in den Brhm. schon nahe genug ist, nunmehr vollständig erreicht und steht als der geborne Repräsentant des Göttlichen selbst da, während auf der anderen Seite die Lage des Çūdra eine höchst gedrückte und traurige ist.

This opinion seems to me in part erroneous. As well known the utmost disorder prevails in the arrangement of the text of the Mān. Dh. Çās., and with the mixed and confused statements which we meet at random through the work it were perhaps well nigh impossible that an opinion other than the above could have been uttered, yet I think after an inspection of the work based on a clear and orderly arrangement of the various ordinances we shall be obliged to modify this view. It is therefore to solve, among others, such important questions as are here involved, that this paper is written. With special regard to the relations between Br. and Ksh. (more particularly the king) I have adopted the following arrangement of the discussion:

1. The statements which concern the four castes in general. 2. Those which concern only the twice born (dvija) castes. 3. The Br., a) his absolute position, b) his position relative to his brother Br., c) his relations with the under castes exclusive of Ksh. 4. The Ksh., a) general regulations for the caste, b) the Ksh. relative to other members of same caste, c) Ksh. and under castes. 5. Vaiçya,

a) general statements for Vaiç., b) Vaiç. and Çūdra. 6. Çūdra, general statements (not included in 3 c) etc.). 7. The Relations between Br. & Ksh., a) general regulations, b) relations of king with Br., c) relation of king with his ministers.

I begin therefore with the general statements in regard to the four castes Br. Ksh. Vaiç. Çūd.

I. The Four castes: A comparison of the relations of the four castes begins naturally with their origin. This subject has however been already so fully discussed in the work quoted above that it would be but useless repetition to enter into the question here. I refer therefore for treatment of this point to Muir Orig. Sk. Texts, Vol. I, p. 35—43, where the contradictions and variations are handled at large and content myself with quoting the few verses relative to the subject without further remark. M. I, 31. For the sake of the growth of the worlds the Lord (prabhuḥ çl. 28) created from his mouth, arm, thigh, and foot (respectively) the Br. the Ksh. the Vaiç. and the Çūd. (Kull. refers to RV. X. 90, 12). The lord ordained also the occupation of these castes. I, 87. For the sake of the preservation of this whole creation the Great and Glorious i. e. Brahmā (prabhuḥ) ordained separate occupations for those born from his mouth, arm, thigh, and foot. (88) As the (occupations and duties) of the Br. he ordained teaching (the veda etc.), studying, making sacrifices for himself and sacrificing for others, giving to others and receiving from others. (89) (He ordained as the occupations and duties) of the Ksh. protection of the people, giving to others, the sacrifice, studying, and avoidance of the sensual passions (vishayeshu aprasakti K. not cultivating the enjoyment of music dance or women). (90) (As those) of the Vaiçya (he ordained) the protection of cattle, giving to others, the sacrifice, studying, trading, lending at interest and agriculture. (91) One occupation the Lord ordained for the Çūdra — to serve without discontent and with complete obedience these (other) castes.

The distinction between the occupations of the four castes is thus stated to be made by the lord as well as the simple distinction between the castes themselves as men. It is worthy of note in this allotment of karmāṇi that the only caste where moral laws are enjoined is that of the Ksh. Ceremonial rites, studying and generosity are ordained for the three upper castes, the one duty of obedience for the Çūd. but the restriction in sensual enjoyment is enjoined only for the military caste.[1]) The right of making sacrifices for others (yājanam) in distinction from private sacrifices (yajanam, ijyā) is here attributed only to the Br. caste. In the second book we have perhaps a reference to the time where every one of the three upper castes was regarded a priest (vipra) of his own family yam . . . çuciṃ vidyān niyata brahmacāriṇam (Brahmacaryopapannam Niruk.) tasmai mām (vidyām) brūhi viprāya. II 114—115. The ancient tone of the verse is shown by a comparison with Nirukta II 4, the latter being apparently a still older version.

We pass to the general ordinances of the law in reference to the four castes. As well known the three upper castes are enjoined to occupy a particular part of India but a Çūdra may live where he pleases, etān dvijātayo deçān saṃçrayeran prayatnataḥ çūdrastu yasmin kasmin vā nivased vṛttikarshitaḥ (II 24)[2]), and from this last word even the Çūdra would seem to be ordinarily confined to the same districts. Among these divisions of the land, two, Brahmâvarta (sarasvatīdṛshadvatyor devanadyor yad antaram) (17) and Brahmarshideça (kurukshetra, matsyāḥ, pañcālāḥ, çūrasenakāḥ) (19) seem to have been noted as the home of the best, in other words the authority-giving dvijāḥ; for we learn of the first: whatever custom has been handed down in that country from the castes and the mixed castes that is called the custom of the good (II 18), cf. I 108 ācāraḥ paramo dharmaḥ çrutyuktaḥ smārta eva ca). It is noteworthy that according to II 18 the mixed castes (sa-antarālāḥ varṇāḥ) are reckoned among the traditionary

1) Prescribed however in general terms as a rule for all castes in X. 63. So Yāj. I. 122.

2) Deçān: namely the lands mentioned in Çl. 17. 19. 21. 22. 23. called Brahmāvartadeça, Brahmarshideça, Madhyadeça, and āryavarta — and the land of the Kṛshṇasāra.

facts together with and having as high authority in settling ācāra as the pure castes. It is also said of the second of these lands that all men on earth could learn their habits from one born in that country. We shall see that it is also noted for its warriors.[1]) The inhabitants of the other two districts seem to have had no such distinction. That a special pride was taken in being born in one district more than in another we see in VIII 273, where the false denial of the land from which a Br. comes is reckoned as great a crime as (or at least classed together with) the crime of denying his learning and high birth. Johäntgen considers this mention of the lands as merely indicative of the originally narrow province in which the law-book first arose.[2])

The four castes are grounded in the veda XII 97 cāturvarṇyam - - vedāt prasiddhyati (as are also the āçramāḥ). The fourfold token of duty is declared to be vedaḥ, smṛtiḥ, sadācāraḥ svasyaca prīyam ātmanaḥ II 12 (so 6) — where the sadācāra, custom of good men, is subordinate in importance to smṛti if we may judge by the position of the words. Twice born are the Br. Ksh. and Vaiç. (dvijātayaḥ) but the Çūdra is ekajātiḥ and na asti tu pañcamaḥ (varṇaḥ) X 4. The four castes seem to be included in a somewhat doubtful passage II 134 Daçābdākhyam paurasakhyam. What this «citizen friendship» is, is not very clear from the text itself. From the connection however it seems to be in regard to the Abhivādana and on the surface the sense seems to be that all citizens are to address each other equally until they are ten years of age. Böhtlingk however interprets this very literally as implying that the friendship of citizens rests on a ten years' ac-

1) VIII 193 v. below.

2) Über das Gesetzbuch des Manu p. 110: Deuten wir nun die symbolische Ausdrucksweise um, so besagt die Stelle (which we have just quoted from the second book) weiter nichts als dass das in dem vorliegenden Werke mitgetheilte Gesetz ursprünglich in jenem kleinen Gebiete zwischen der Sarasvatī und Dṛshadvatī in Geltung gewesen sei, dass sich dasselbe aber in weiterem Kreise Anerkennung verschafft und nun als für alle Indier bindend hingestellt werde. But cf. Weber Vorl. p. 112 Note.

quaintance, thus severing the clause from the connection with the foregoing rules. [1]) But I think if we compare a passage in Gautama (VI 15 flg.) we shall see that this çloka is said only of address and that sakhya is to be rendered «equality» merely in this respect. For Gautama though not agreeing precisely in the expression yet gives the years as the same for citizens, artists, and çrotriya. Here however the rule is laid down that fellow citizens who are ten years older [2]) are to be addressed with bhoḥ, bhavan etc. and we may indeed transfer this directly as interpretation of the manavic text; for the apparent interpretation of ten years of age fits badly to the other characters and the upanayana of the Br. taking place at 8 years would even destroy the first, though the general term 10 years is thus loosely used in the next çloka. In view of the agreement with the text of Gautama B.'s translation [3]) will scarcely stand. The general statement in M. which is all inclusive would however accepting G.'s rule as an explanation exclude Çūdra on account of bhavan. [?]

Maṇgalyam should be the name of the Br. balānvitam that of the Ksh. dhanasaṃyuktam that of the Vaiç. and jugupsitam that of the Çūdra II 31. also 32, çarmavad should be the name of the Br. Rakshāsamanvitam that of the Ksh. (rājan) pushṭisaṃyuktam that of the Vaiç. and praishyasaṃyuktam that of the Çūdra. Kull. designates the second class of names as upapadāni. [4])

A vipra is purified by water reaching to the breast hṛdgābhiḥ (adbhiḥ), a Ksh. by water reaching to his throat

1) The other translators accept Kull.'s simple daçabhir abdair-jyeshṭatve sati api sakhyam âkhyâyate. Jones: Fellow citizens are equal for ten years. Loiseleur Deslongchamps: L'égalité n'est pas détruite entre citoyens d'une ville par une différence d'âge de dix ans.

2) The words daçavarshavṛddhaḥ pauraḥ do not require more than the meaning ten years old but as this can not be the case in 16 we are entitled to the interpretation of the commentator. That simple greeting is meant follows from 14.

3) B.'s translation is found: Böhtlingk, Zur Kritik und Erklärung verschiedener Indischer Werke in Mélanges Asiatiques. Tome VII p. 448.

4) W. in Ind. Stud. X s. 21 gives Pār. 1, 17 des Br. Namen endet auf çarman, der des Ksh. auf varman, der des Vaiç. auf gupta.

(kaṇṭhagābhiḥ), a Vaiç. by water reaching the palate — taken into the mouth prāçitābhiḥ Kull. antarāsyapravishṭābhiḥ Yāj. I 21 tāluyābhiḥ and a Çūdra (also a woman acc. to (as in M. V, 139) Yāj.) by spṛshṭābhiḥ — antataḥ. II 62.

The purification of the Br. (upanītasapiṇḍamaraṇe K.) takes place in ten days, that of the Ksh. in 12, that of Vaiç. in 15 — that of the Çūd. in a month. (V 83). Yāj. III 22 does not mention the Br. but gives the purification of the others as here with the addition that Nyāyavartinaḥ (Çūdrāḥ) require only fifteen days of purification, thus the same for a worthy Çūd. as for Vaiç. So in Manu V 140 in vapanam and the accompanying purification. After a religious ceremony, kṛtakriyaḥ, a vipra is purified by touching water, a Ksh. by touching a horse (vāhana) or weapon, a Vaiç. by touching his goad or reins, a Çūdra by touching his stick, yashṭi, V 99.

The priest, vipra, swears by his truth, the Ksh. by his horse or weapons, the Vaiç. by his cattle, seed or by gold, a Çūd. by all wickedness, sarvaih pātakaiḥ VIII 113. K. to Çūd. sarvāṇi me pātakāni syur iti evam çāpayet. To compare with this is VIII 88 also said of witnesses: when the judge calls on the witnesses he says to the Brahm.: speak, brūhi, to the Ksh.: speak the truth, satyam brūhi, to the Vaiç.: by cattle seed or gold, and to a Çūdra: by all wickedness. K. explains the latter half in this place Govījasuvarṇāpahāre yat pāpam tat tava anṛtābhidhāne syād iti evam vaiçyam (pṛcchet) — sarvaiḥ vakshyamāṇapāpaiḥ sambadhyase yadi mṛshā vadasi iti (çūdram) pṛcchet. This is in order to connect with the following çlokas and bring in harmony w. 102. but it is plain that this line does not belong here, the explanation can scarcely be made out of the simple Inst. of the text, the construction is changed, the meaning must be extended, the line is exactly the same as in 113 where it has a good sense, and finally it is here illogical; for we are informed in the preceding verse that it is the *twice born* (dvijāḥ) whom the judge is addressing. The criticism rises naturally therefore that a confusion has arisen between Çl. 88 and 113, the line belonging properly only to the latter,[1]) and is therefore perhaps a gloss.

Let one address a Br. with the word kuçalam, a kshatrabandhu with anāmayam, a Vaiç. with kshemam and a Çūdra with ārogyam. II 127.[2]) The Ksh. may ward off imminent danger by the strength of his arm, a Vaiç. or Çūd. by his property, but a Br. by prayers and offerings XI 34. Speech is the weapon of the Br., vākçastram Brāhmaṇasya (33) (cf. below) cf. Mbhâ XII 432. — The punishment which the Br. may inflict is that of the voice, of Ksh. that of arm, of Vaiç. that of gifts, a Çūdra has none. (Nirdaṇḍaḥ Çūdra ucyate).

The tapas of the Br. is jñānam, of the Ksh. rakshaṇam, of the Vaiç. vārttā, of the Çūd. sevanam XI 236, as to the tapas of the Br. cf. II 166. The study of the veda is mentioned as the highest tapas also IV 147. They say this (study of veda) is the highest duty — every other is secondary. In killing a Ksh. a fourth part of the penalty for killing a Br. is ordained, in killing a Vaiç. an eighth part and in killing a virtuous Çūd. a sixteenth part XI 127. This regulation is given without distinction of caste of the slayer. That the deed here mentioned is intentional murder is indicated by 128 akāmatas tu etc. in opposition to this çl. Yāj. III 266—267 gives also an uncertain subject (pumān). The superiority of the vipra is derived from his knowledge that of the Ksh. from his manliness that of the Vaiç. from his wealth in corn etc. that of the Çūd. from his birth i. e. age. II 155[3]) cf. 154. Na hāyanair na palinair na vittena na bandhubhiḥ, ṛshayaç cakrire dharmam — yo 'nūcānaḥ sa no mahān.[4])

In burials the Çūd. is carried out by the southern gate

1) In VIII 256 the deciders of boundaries are sworn by their good deeds.

2) So Āpast. except anashṭam for kshemam 1. 4. 14. 28. — Gaut. V 41. 42 ārogya for Vaiç. and Çūd.

3) Āpast. uses this expression (1. 1. 1. 3) which is here applied to the Çūd. janmataḥ of all the castes, where it means birth, teshām (the four castes) pūrvo pūrvo janmataḥ çreyān.

4) Cf. B. Sprüche 3508 & 9.

the Vaiç. by the western, the Ksh. by the northern, the Br. by the eastern V 92. There are seven vīttāgamā dharmyāḥ or honest methods of obtaining a living. These are given by Manu without distinction of caste. Inheritance (Dāyaḥ), Reception (or seizure) (Lābhaḥ), Purchase (Krayaḥ) Conquest (Jāyaḥ), money gained by lending and agriculture (prayogaḥ and karmayogaḥ), and acceptance of presents from good people (Satpratigrahaḥ) X 115. Kull. assigns dāyaḥ lābhaḥ krayaḥ to the first three or even all the castes — jayaḥ to the Ksh. prayogaḥ and karmayogaḥ to the Vaiç. and pratigrahaḥ to the Br. There are given again in the next çloka, 116, ten jīvanahetavaḥ limited by Kull. to āpat cases (so Yāj. III 42). They are vidyā çilpam bhṛti sevā gorakshyam vipaṇiḥ kṛshiḥ dhṛtiḥ bhaikshyam kusīdam in which any detailed relation of these provisions cannot be found since the occupation of the Ksh. fails entirely (The provisions of Yāj. are not more definite, he also restricts to cases of necessity apparently also only for the Br.). As the text stands the very extraordinary conclusion must be drawn that the Br. is not excluded from servitude (so also Yāj. if we bring the çl. in connection with the foregoing). Kull. however supports this opinion and says that a mode of life forbidden in time of prosperity may be assumed in time of distress, so the Br. is permitted at such times both bhṛti and sevā and the other jīvanāni — teaching of the veda however, he remarks, is not permitted without restriction but he may (always āpadi) teach anyone philosophy, remedies for poison etc. in order to support himself. In çl. 117 we find a restriction that we may add in this connection. The Br. and even the Ksh. should not make money by lending but dharmārtham they may *give* a small interest even to a wicked man. Cf. Yāj. I 132 Let him not be a thief nor a money lender. Condemned also in VIII 102 (not āpadi). The Br. who tend cattle, who engage in trade, who are workmen servants or usurers he (king or judge) should handle as Çūdras — (K. prakṛta sākshipraçne çūdravat pṛcchet) — the case is of witnesses. Banishment without restriction of caste where therefore all may be understood is enjoined as punishment in IX 225.

Heretics and such as live by an improper business (as well as players, men of bad habits, cruel men, dealers in spirits) let the king quickly banish. VIII 284 If one break the skin (of another) he is to be fined one hundred. So if he draw blood; if he wound a muscle six nishka and for breaking a bone he is to be banished. Kull. says this is only to be understood of those of the same caste not of the injury of a Br. by a Çūdra, as one sees from the unimportance of the penalty. Against this construction however we shall have to accept this as an universal law; for from the connection we should be led to suppose the exact opposite of what Kull. says (v. 281—83) where utkṛshṭa and apakṛshṭa are expressly named and Yāj. in the corresponding ordinance of his law book (II 218—219) says nothing of equal castes giving only as subject the indefinite naraḥ. The lessening of the punishment for darçane asṛjaḥ by a third (64) (paṇas) instead of an hundred shows the later character of his law. The banishment is not mentioned at all by him. Another passage in M. (VIII 219—220) may also be cited here — whoever among the unions (samghāḥ) in town or country having made an agreement becomes false to it, him let the king banish from his realm, and seizing the breaker of a contract let (the king) fine him four suvarṇaḥ six nishka and a çatamāna of silver. This law of punishment let a just king establish among the unions of town or country who break their compacts. The samūha of 221 is equivalent to the saṃgha. It seems as though the second çloka were a modification of the first in settlement of the punishment, and may therefore be supposed to be of later date.

Entirely without restriction of caste in Manu are the well known judgements of God described in the eighth book. The judges (if the swearing by truth etc. (v. above) is not sufficient) must cause the witness to hold fire, or sink in the water, or touch the heads of wife and son i. e. appeal to the Gods. VIII 114, 115. Yāj., who gives a longer description and describes the use for the same purpose of scales, and poison, and consecrated water (mentioning also the ploughshare trial) Yāj. II 99[1]) which show a later development of this practice, restricts the general use we find in Manu, specifying the scales for women, children, old men, blind, lame, brāhmans, and sick people, while fire, water, and poison are for the Çūdra. In Manu however is there not only no such restriction but there is the strongest proof that all castes are included in this regulation; for immediately preceding stands the çloka which we have quoted above in which each caste is expressly mentioned — and the last half of 114 is really only an extension of 113. So that it would be wellnigh impossible to escape the conclusion that agnim vā hārayed enam contains as personal object any one caste as well as any other mentioned in 113. All the four castes are mentioned by name in the preceding çloka nor is any change made as the subject here. Conclusive proof moreover is the fact that the example cited in the next çloka, to prove the justness of the trial is that of a Br. viz. Vatsa cf. 116.

Among the notes of the four castes in general we may add the description of the «Seven-limbed kingdom» IX 294—296 as the relative worth of the members are here spoken of. The çloka reads svāmyamātyau, puram, rāshṭram, koçadaṇḍau suhṛt tathā | sapta prakṛtayo hy etāḥ «saptāñgaṃ rājyam» ucyate. (So Yāj. I 352 svāmyamātyau, jano durgam koço, daṇḍaḥ . . . mitrāṇi) — (The king) himself, his ministers (Brahmans), the people of the city and the general kingdom, the treasury, the army, and the allies form the kingdom of seven members. Between puram and rāshṭram seems to lie a difference of the residence of the king and his general realm, the land.

The Br. are here represented, they are the ministers, and the Ksh., they are the army (daṇḍa — Stenzler regarding the following çloka translates in the corresponding passage in Yāj. with «Strafe».) The Vaiç. and rest of the

1) Schlagintweit in his interesting essay «Über die Gottesurtheile der Indier» has neglected to mention Yāj. under ploughshare giving only an extract from the description of Hiuen Thsang (fr. St. Julien). Under this head we must too reckon in Manu VIII 108. distinctly a supernatural decision. To the oath proof we may add VIII 190.

folk are united in the terms puram and rāshṭram. The next çl. says: each of these seven elements of the realm is more important than the next in order, (Yathākramamṃ pūrvam pūrvañ gurutaram) if it be injured[1]) but, 296, supported like the tridaṇḍaḥ the realm has no part which excells another in excellence of attributes. This means simply when the realm is at peace and the public weal unendangered all the members as a whole work with equal benefit to the others, in case of calamity however it would be better to sacrifice the last named in order till the king be reached. In consequence we are to understand that the army is to be sacrificed rather than that the realm should be ruined or the city destroyed, and the (brahmanic) ministers are to be sacrificed before the king. The verses 215,. 216, are not paralleled as is 214 in Yāj.

The king tries all cases of law in the order of the castes (varṇakrameṇa) VIII 24. Among those who are not to serve as witnesses are the çrotriya and the liñgastha (= Brahmacārin) the Sañgebhyo vinirgataḥ and also the king VIII 65.

Certain of the Br. were therefore excluded (as Kull. explains that there attention might not be distracted while engaged in religious duties). The other three castes are without exception liable to be called upon (excepting the king from the Ksh. caste) Kshatraviṭçūdrayonayaḥ . . . sākshyam arhanti VIII 62 — and men of all castes who are fitted i. e. except unworthy and the çrotriya etc. of 65. āptā sarveshu varṇeshu kāryāḥ kāryeshu sākshiṇaḥ (63). Slaves old men etc. (and 65, 66, 67) who are usually forbidden are allowed on failure of proper witnesses, among whom are the çishya (= liñgastha of 65) bandhu, dāsa and bhṛtaka or even (69) anyone who knows the facts may be witness when the occurrence has taken place in a house, or wood, or at a death — which takes away all restrictions, and finally a restriction is given that (if possible) women should be witnesses for women, twice born men of like caste for the twice born, and a Çūdra for the Çūdra, moreover the outcast only should be witness for his equal (68). Kull.

remarks that in the absence of those of the same, men of other castes may serve as witnesses, and quotes Yāj. (II 69) yathājāti yathāvarṇam *sarve sarveshu vā smṛtāḥ*. In conflicting testimony that of the plurality is to be accepted — if the number on each side is the same that of the good, and in case of guṇidvaidham where both parties are virtuous that of the highest twice born among the witnesses, i. e. Brahmans VIII 73 so Yāj. II 78 — for dvijottamāḥ, guṇavattamāḥ.

Eightfold is the sin (kilbisham) of a Çūd. in theft, sixteenfold that of the Vaiç., thirty-twofold that of the Ksh., sixty-fourfold that of the Br. (or even 100 or 128) because he knows the nature of the crime VIII 337 338, («Kilbisham» can mean either his moral crime or the legal punishment.) cf. Mhbhâ. XII 1272—3 — catushpādātmakalo Dharmo Br. pādāvakṛshṭo rājanye etc. In paying debts when the debtor is unable to make full payment the three under castes are obliged to work out the payment, the Br. however is permitted to wait and pay gradually. IX 229 the castes of Ksh. Vaiç. and Çūd. being unable (to pay) the fine shall free themselves by work from debt (ānṛṇyaṃ karmaṇā gacchet) a vipra however shall give by instalments (çanaiḥ çanaiḥ). In this çloka the payment can be either that of a legal fine or a private debt. The latter seems to be the case in the similar verse VIII 177. The debtor should pay the creditor (samaṃ kuryāt) by work, if of the same or of a lower caste, but a superior in caste (çreyān) shall give çanaiḥ. The logical conclusion of this çloka would be that the Br. if in debt with a Br. is tacitly obliged to pay it as the others by his labour. Kull. adds Brāhmaṇetara and supports this exclusion of the Br. from the universality of the expression samajātiḥ through a quotation from Kātyāyana: Let (the king) cause the Ksh. Viç. Çūd. being of equal or lower caste to pay by their work. He might also have quoted Yāj. II 43: Let the king compel work for money-indebtedness in the case of a man of lower caste without money; but a Br. when moneyless shall pay çanaiḥ . . . . yathâ udayam.

The four castes are mutually responsible for insults.

If a Ksh. insult a Br. he is to be fined 100 (paṇas), the Vaiç. 150 or 200 (with consideration of the lightness or severity of the insult Kull.) and the Çūd. deserves vadha, VIII 267, and further (268) the Br. shall pay 50 on reviling a Ksh. 25 if he revile a Vaiç. and 12 in the case of a Çūd. (269) — 12 is the fine for a slight on one of the same caste among the twice born — this should however be doubled if the words of reproach are such as should not be spoken (this refers acc. to Kull. also to 267—268). No fine is here enjoined for insults from Ksh. to Çūd. or Ksh. to Vaiç. (for Vaiç. & Çūd. s. below), cf. Yāj. II 206 daṇḍapraṇayanam kāryam varṇa jātyuttarādharaiḥ, and 207 prātilomyāpādeshu dviguṇatriguṇā damāḥ, varṇānām ānulomyena tasmād ardhārdhahānitaḥ. Thus Yāj. gives only through general rule the right of the Çūdra to be justified by the court whereas Manu gives a settled fine which the Br. must pay as well in case of a Çūdra as in that of Ksh. & Vaiç.[1])

Muir I 41. 42 has already remarked that in the distribution of the castes among the states of sattva rajas and tamas in XII 40 flg. the Vaiç. has no place and that kings, purohita and Ksh. are placed together, and besides distinctions are made in the priests' conditions not explainable by their real position.

The theological speculations of the same book in çl. 70—72 group the castes together as follows. If the members of the castes without necessity depart from their respective occupations they enter sinful (men) and become slaves under their enemies. By neglect of their duties a Br. becomes after death an Ulkâmukha, a Ksh. a Kaṭapûtana, a Vaiç. a maitrākshajyotika and a Çūd. a Cailāçaka.[2])

These functions give but little preference to any one of these spirits (vomit-eater, impurity-eater, rotten-food-eater, and moth-eater), but as far as choice in such diet can extend the Çūd. seems to meet with the most agreeable fate, probably on the principle elsewhere enunciated that the best instructed deserves, if he sin, the greatest penalty.

1) Acc. to Gautama XII 13 the Br. is in this case to pay nothing though the fines for insulting Ksh. & Vaiç. agree w. M.

2) Cf. for Br. the similar epithet in III 109 vāntāçī.

A passage in the III Bk. (196—198) in which the Manes of the castes are mentioned closes with the parentage of these manes (somapāḥ of vipra, havirbhūjaḥ of Ksh. ājyapāḥ of Vaiç. and sukālinaḥ of Çūd.). In which the somapāḥ are presented as sons of Kavi (Kull. kaver, bhṛgoḥ) the havirbhūjaḥ or havishmantaḥ as sons of Angir, the ājyapāḥ as sons of Pulastya and the sukālinaḥ as sons of Vasishṭha.

Why Vasishṭha should thus be appointed as progenitor of the Çūdras does not appear clear as the name is mentioned with respect in VIII 140 although there as a lawgiver, and here as a demigod. The name appears in I 35 as Prajāpatis. These are the regulations in Manu which include specifically or generally all the castes.[1]) With regard to the latter cases it were wrong if we in spite of the irregular arrangement of the text refused to apply a restriction which plainly and connectedly limits the bearing of the universal formula. In spite of this again, however, we must acknowledge that passages occur in Manu in regard to the four castes implying or containing injunctions to which the upper caste or castes were liable, which injunctions were afterward disregarded, annulled, or restricted by the later Law-book. (cf. above the discussion of X 115—116. VIII 284. VIII 114. 115. VIII 177. VIII 268).

II. The three Twice born Castes.

Among the occupations peculiar (to the three castes) the most respected are, for a Br., studying the Veda, for a Ksh., Protecting, and for a Vaiçya, vārttā (keeping herds, agriculture, trading), X 80.

The Cūḍākarma (or cutting off the hair of the child) of the twice born takes place in the first or the third year according to the Çruti. II 35. (Kull. In 1st or 3rd year after birth as the regulation depends in its variations on the family usage. So Yāj. yathâkulam I 12).

The Keçāntaḥ is ordained for the sixteenth year in case of a Br. for the rājanyabandhu in the twenty-second year and for

1) The passage in I 28 which seems to imply a continuity of the same duties is either to be taken simply with 27 or refers to future award with XII 81.

the Vaiç. in two more, II 65. Yāj. gives only the 16th year I 36. At the same relative age the ceremony sāvitrī may be performed. In the 8th year from the birth of a Br., in the 11th of a Ksh. (rājan), in the 12th of a Viç is the upanāyanam. If the vipra desires religious superiority it is to be performed in the 5th year, if the Ksh. desires power in the 6th, and if the Vaiç. desires wealth in the 8th year II 36. 37; but later than the 16th year the sāvitrī should not be delayed, not later than the 22nd for a kshatriyabandhu, nor later than the 24th for the Viç. (II 38). Later than this the three castes if asamskṛtāḥ become sāvitrīpatitā vrātyāḥ (39). These outcasts are further described (40) as āryavigarhitāḥ and the Br. are enjoined to have nothing to do with them.

There is however a means of salvation for those who have failed to enter the caste order at the appointed time; this is in Yāj. I 14 and I 37—38 implied by the words vrātyastomādṛte,[1]) unless they have performed the rites for the outcast, this is again, though not here implied, enjoined by Manu in XI 192 «Such twice born as have not heard the sāvitrī (gāyatrī) according to law let the (king — assembly [?]) cause to perform three kṛcchrā (penances) and have the ceremony of upanayanam performed».[2])

The clothing of the scholars of the three castes is also different — anupûrveṇa — Let the Brahmacāriṇah wear skins of the kṛshṇa, ruru, or goat — also hemp, flax, and wool according to their caste II 41.[3]) The mekhalā of the vipra is thrice twisted and smooth made of muñja, that of the Ksh. of mūrvā a bow string, that of the Vaiç. of hemp II 42 or 43. When the muñja (jyā) is not to be obtained the cord should be of kuça, açmāntaka, and balbaja, thrice twisted with one, three, or five knots. The upavītam of the vipra is of cotton going over the shoulder (ūrdhvavṛtam), a Ksh.'s of hemp-thread, and a Vaiç.'s

1) Yāj. gives the years as M. adds yathākulam as opinion of eke.

2) Kṛcchrā Kull. equals prājāpatya v. XI 212 performed by eating three days only in the morning, three only in evening, three only what is offered without asking, three complete fasting.

3) Cf. for these restrictions Weber Ind. Stud. X 21—23. In case of the clothing the Br. according to Pār. Gobh. seems to have a choice.

of wollen thread II 44. These are mentioned by Yāj. without restrictions of kind I 29. The staves of the castes like the sacred cord girdle and clothing are also anupūrveṇa (45) the Br. should have a staff of bilva or palāça wood the Ksh. from vaṭa or khadira wood. The Vaiç. from pīlu or udumbara (46). The Br.'s staff should reach his hair, the Ksh.'s his brow, the Vaiç.'s his nose.

The twice born have three births! The first birth of the twice born is in the beginning from the mother, the second is through the binding of the sacred cord (mauñjibandhane) and the third is in the sacrificial consecration, yajñadīkshāyām, II 169 çruticodanāt. Yāj. I 39 gives only the first two.

Among the twice born this (bhaikshacaraṇam) i. e. daily begging, is only to be performed by the Br. This act is not permitted the Ksh. and Vaiç. II 190. The student must beg for food from one of his female relations, a duty enjoined on all on entering the caste; but the highest of the twice born, the Br., must speak bhavati at the beginning, the Ksh. in the middle, the Vaiç. at the end. II 49.[1])

To certain among the twice born the udakakriyā (at burial services) is forbidden .— aside from those who as heretics or wrong doers lose this right the following are deprived from the condition of their position; after remarking V 88 that the Brahmacārins can bring no such offering Manu adds: Vṛthāçaṅkarajātānām pravrajyāsu ca tishṭhatāmnivarteta udakakriyā. The water-offering should not be performed in the case of those who live wrongly or are of mixed caste (Kull. jātaçabdaḥ pratyekam abhisambadhyate) 89 and of pravrajyāsu tishṭhatām — this can only mean «of those who have taken up a wandering life», the pious wandering Br. beggar. This is not found in Yāj.'s list III 6 (pāshaṇḍyanāçritāh stands parallel to M. pāshaṇḍamāçritāḥ!) 90.[2]) Acc. to Yāj. II 235 the pravrajita are to be as carefully excluded as the Çūd. from the daivam pitryam. As a fem.

1) Ind. Stud. X 22 from Pār. Āçv. Kauç. (also Yāj. I 29. 30. Āpast. 1. 1. 3. 28) Kull. bhavati bhikshām dehi iti, bhikshām bhavati dehiiti, bhikshām dehi bhavati iti.

2) In Yāj. a dvandva comp. but the agreement is strange.

this has been thought to refer to Buddh. beggar women in VIII 363, the expression pravrajitā being used in the pregnant sence of the old Norse «farandi kona». (Cf. carantī in V 90). S. Weber Vorl. 299 Note.

Ten are they who may be instructed. The son of the ācārya, an obedient (one), one who gives knowledge, a just one, a pure one, an apt one, a powerful one, a giver of wealth, a good one, and his own II 109. No preference of caste is given here except in the first case. It is curious that Yāj. omits from his text (I 28) the ācāryaputraḥ, the çuçrūshuḥ (an epithet usually reserved for the Çūdra) and svaḥ. The latter may mean his son by a low woman, i. e. may belong to a mixed caste. (Anasūyaka in Y. is perhaps the equivalent of çuçrūshu of M.). As to a distinction in regard and respect toward the sons cf. II 207. The sons of the Guru are to be treated with the same respect as the Guru, or not, according as they are or are not āryan — which may mean simply worthy of honour or may refer to completeness in caste, for the sons of the Br. by women of under castes are not respected.

The twice born man (dvija) who unwearedly repeats apart a thousand times (daily) (the praṇava sāvitrī and vyāhṛti) is in a month released from even a great sin like a snake from his slough; and the Br. Ksh. and Vaiç. come to scorn among the good if they do not perform the sacrifices punctually, and if they neglect these ṛk verses. II 79. 80 also 82: Who goes over unwearedly day by day for three years (the Om vyāhṛti and sāvitrī) enters the highest Brahm with a nature like the wind and a body of air.[1]) This is a general sentence for all the twice born.

Among the three upper castes the Br. appears as the supporter in time of need. The Br. should support a Ksh. and Vaiç. where they have no means of livelihood, making them do their own business without injuring them. If however he cause saṃskṛtā dvijāḥ to perform the work of

1) For the idea expressed in khamūrtimān v. farther in M. III 93 tejomūrtiḥ and IV 243 khaçarīrī and II 232 dīpyamānaḥ, all used of the being after death.

a slave (dāsyam) through covetousness, when they do not wish to, he shall be fined six hundred by the king VIII 411—412. This is not distinctly stated by Yāj. and he gives only the rule varṇānām ānulomyena dāsyam na pratilomataḥ (II 183), where this case would not be excluded or at the most a balāddāsīkṛta is released, but no fine is mentioned for the enslaver (182). Neither the Br. the Rājanya nor the Vaiç. should drink the surā, since surā is malam annānām and wickedness is also called malam XI 94. The injunction of a new saṃskāra is given if the twice born have unintentionally eaten faeces urine or what has been touched by surā, XI 151, so Yāj. III 255.

Which ever one of the twice born flies upon the Br. vadhakāmyayā he shall pass an hundred years in the hell Tāmisra, and striking him even with a piece of grass, angrily and with intention, he is born in twenty one despicable births IV 165—166. We shall see that this is in another part represented as a penalty for all without distinction of caste. Among the general rules for slander the twice born are included in VIII 275, one who defames his .... Guru and gives not the right of way to the Guru shall be fined 100, thus restrictive to the three upper castes.

IIIa. The Brahman. The Br. is defined XI 35 as an arranger of sacrifices, vidhātar, one who corrects, one who proclaims (expiation etc. and (rules of) duty, Kull.) and one who is friendly, maitrin. He is called a Br. Cf. II 87 maitro Brāhmaṇa ucyate (prayer is his best work) also VI 66: equalminded toward all beings; the sign (of caste) is not productive of virtue.[1]) Cf. also Y. III 65 Na āçramaḥ kāraṇam dharme and also Y. I 200. This broad definition of the Br. presents him simply in the light of the man having duties to perform and moral obligations as a man. The Br. is regarded throughout the codex of Manu as of double nature, on the one hand we have a godlike perhaps divine nature before us, on the other a man liable as other men to ills,

1) Cf. VI 8. Syād dānto maitraḥ samāhitaḥ. Could the frequent use of this term be brought in connection with the name of the Saṃhita to which Schroeder assigns the manavic school?

and liable to punishment if inflicting them. To separate the godlike side from the mortal side is often easy, if we consider that the boasts of the Br. divinity stand for the most part isolated, without logical effect upon his actions, and when his more than mortal side is expressly stated to exalt him above all mortal laws the verses which thus proclaim his godliness are almost always practically annulled, either directly or tacitly, as soon as the more precise discussion of the point is given. The Br. as divinity is mentioned in the following passages. XI 85. The Br. is by his very nature Devānām Daivatam — he is the authority of the world — for the ground of things is in Brahm, (Brahmātra Kull. «in the Veda»). — Extracts from I 98—101 show the Br. as the lord of all beings and above all human law of right: utpattir eva viprasya mūrtir dharmasya . . sa hi dharmārtham utpanno brahmabhūyāya kalpate — pṛthivyāmadhijāyate, īçvaraḥ sarvabhūtānām dharmakoçasya guptaye — and after declaring that the Br. is born for the protection of justice we are informed, sarvaṃ svam brāhmaṇasya idam — yat kiñcij jagatīgatam — — svam eva brāhmaṇo bhuṅkte svaṃ vaste svam dadāti ca, ānṛçaṃsyād brāhmaṇasya bhuñjate hi itare janāḥ. Although born over the world, and possessing, according to this çloka, every thing in it, and so partaking of a godlike character, yet a direct union with the godhead is not here predicated of the Br. The wild extravagance of these çlokas Kull. was obliged to temper to reason. He adds: svam iva svam na tu svam eva brāhmaṇasya api Manunā steyasya vakshyamānatvāt (to çl. 100) in which lies the kernel of the right explanation of the many inconsistences in regard to this point.

As the Br. is here īçvaraḥ sarvabhūtānām so he is sarvasya sargasya prabhuḥ through his birth from the uppermost member, through his superiority, and through his holding the supreme spirit (or Veda) I 93. Cf. Y. I 198. 199 and M. I 94. The self-existent produced the Br. from his mouth to uphold the havya and kavya and protect the world. Kull. adds that the Br. is also lord of castes through his Saṃskāra (M. X 3).

The Br. is also Agni (so is the king) [1]; for at a sacrifice described in III 212 we have the sacrificer placing the havis in the hand of the vipra if there is no fire in which to throw it, for the vipras who understand the mantras declare fire and the twice born (here Br.) as the same, Yo hi agniḥ sa dvijaḥ.

The passage in which the godlike character of the Br. is expressed in the strongest language is in IX 313 flg. He is here represented as Brahm, and the creation is attributed to him. After remarking that a king must never make a Br. angry, Manu says (313): The Br. if angry could kill him with all his forces — (314) by whom the all devouring fire, the undrinkable sea, the waning and the waxing moon (the soma) are made [2] — who would not perish if he angered these (315)? Those who if enraged could produce other worlds and rulers of worlds and gods and not gods — who could prosper injuring these (316)? — by whom the gods and worlds are — — who could injure these — — (317) learned or unlearned the Br. is a great divinity — etc., 318—319, closing with the declaration that Br. are every where to be honoured, being param daivatam. If we examine these passages in which the superiority of the Br. is asserted we shall notice that only two directly represent the Br. in distinction from the other castes as the incorporation of the divinity and indeed these passages are the only ones in Manu in which such an assertion is met. The two are the one last quoted IX 313 flg. and XI 85. Examining the other passages we find that the dvija is represented as fire but evidently not because the dvija as incarnation of the divine therefore include the Agni but simply because he is the representative of the one god Agni in whose service he stand — and this passage may perhaps be still better construed, since it is openly a quotation from the philosophical speculation, as a mere reference to the fire itself as an element, in which among others the being of man is often enough resolved by the philosophers of the Upanishads. Again, the passage we have quoted from the first book does not in any manner or way assume absolute godhead for the Br. He is born over the earth, lord of creation, lord of all beings; but this is a mere assertion of his right of possession, as we see from the following verses, and the içvara, lord, is in no sense a necessary indication of divine, but here plainly one of temporal power, for the protection of justice; and when we read that the birth of the vipra is per se an incorporation of Dharma or Justice it is not as Jones translates «an Incarnation of Dharma the God of Justice» in the sense that this «God» and the Br. are one and the same, but simply that the Br. stands upon earth as the representative of Justice and so dharmārtham in the same passage. The meaning of godhead here is no more to be extracted from this passage than when we read that the teacher is to the pupil the mūrti of Brahm — that this is representative and not incarnation is shown by the fact that the passage where these words occur (II 225—226, v. below) declare at the same time the father is the mūrti of Prajāpati in which case we must accept the father (and also mother) represented as incarnations of deities.[1]) This is then too strong an expression, and we have absolutely nothing in the passage from which we can deduce the divinity which in the IX book is distinctly predicated. It is therefore of extreme importance for an understanding of this point to examine carefully this passage which stands so boldly opposed to the general statements on this head. I am convinced that an examination will show the passage does not in the least belong to the original work. Not to speak of the passage being somewhat forcibly brought into this connection, in which (assuming it to be a later addition to the work) it were easily accounted for as a sort of vainglorying intended to set off that of the king which immediately precedes — not adducing this as an argument, on account of the oft repeated want of connection between the various parts of the work, there are the following grounds for disbelief in the right of this fragment to lay claim to being a genuine part of the book in which it is found. First, in general, the ninth book has a large number of later pieces received into the original — Stenzler remarked this already in Ind. Stud. I. It is, therefore, in a part of the work which we are not ready to accept without distrust as entirely genuine. The style of the verses in this passage has no parallel elsewhere in Manu. The rhetorical effect aimed at by the frequent repetitions of the same form of expression — ko na naçyet — kaḥ . . . samṛdhnuyāt — ko hiṃçyāt — is entirely foreign to the style elsewhere found in the Dhçs. and reminds us involuntarily of the Mbhā. Again: Sarvabhakshya as epithet of Agni, apeyaçca mahodadhiḥ, the adj. as well as the substantive, kshayin of the moon (soma), and the adevā are all foreign, and belong in part also to Mbhā. Further, we may add that the idea expressed in avidvāṃçca eva vidvāṃçca Br. daivatam mahat contradicts the whole tenor and spirit of the manavic law and is contradicted in half a dozen passages in the Dhçs. (compare VII 85, III 142, III 97, II 157, II 118, II 126, VI 31, XII 114.) On comparing moreover with çl. 314 the note to spruch 5582 we see that the verse is variously modified, cf. also sp. 4223 to çloka 317.[1]) We seek moreover in vain for a similar tirade even in the later Dhçs. of Yāj. From all these reasons it will be scarcely too bold a statement to say that this passage is a later addition to the Dharmaçāstram of Manu and apparently affixed to the original text at a period later than the composition of the Dh.çās. of Yāj. and belongs much more to the character of the epic poetry. Excluding therefore this text as an unjustified addition to the Dhçs. we are left with one passage which asserts that the Br. is the godhead, and this meaning we do not attempt to deny the words quoted above from XI 85. Brāmaṇaḥ . . . . Devānām daivatam — for the word daivatam occurs elsewhere in Manu where it evidently means divinity — (though Kull. here translates, pūjyaḥ) — but though it may be pertinent to ask if a single çloka in a whole Dharmaçāstram can be accepted as proving a point, yet, as the verse stands, it must be admitted; for I know no grounds which can condemn it from the text except that it is elsewhere contradicted, and such a proof can in Manu only be adduced to strengthen, not to create disbelief, since, as already remarked, this is forbidden by the character of the work. It is not assumed, however, that the Br. has not something more in his being than what is found in the other castes. He is represented for instance as purity itself in X 102, and for his exalted station above others we may quote I 96, where he is represented as the logical head of created beings. The living are the best of all things, of the living, those endowed with sense, of these, man, of men, the Br. As lord, īça, of all cf. IX 243—45 cf. also as adhipati VIII 37 v. below. And we are told that the Br. after study, penance, and so forth, in the last stage of life (anena kramayogeṇa) param Brahmādhigacchati VI 85; but it is this fact, that the Br. advances slowly and only through a set path of discipline to union with the godhead, that gives the sharpest contradiction to the assumption that he is in and through himself the personification of that Brahm which he is here and elsewhere represented as striving after. [1])

One power rules the Br. as firmly and as unswervingly as the other castes — a power which is indeed nothing more than a reverential submission to the dictates of the earlier Br. themselves, but which assumes almost a personal might in the adjustment of all questions relative to discipline and ordinary action, and which, almost objectified by the later Br., excludes them entirely (this is the theory) from a free exercise of personal inclination on any point in which this power has given its dicta. This is the *Ācāra* — the sacred uncontradicted binding might of custom

1) The Br. enters Brahm through devout meditation, dhyāyayogena VI 79, so 81 *gradually* he enters into Brahm, also obedience to the ten commandments (VI 93) is a necessary preliminary. So in XII 102 Brahmabhūyāya kalpate — the use of this word as meaning is fitted for i. e. by degrees, is illustrated by VII 23 and VIII 353.

and of those rules which have been forever acted upon, and disobedience of which is represented as little less than a sin against religion itself. The Ācāra is in fact the outward expression of religion, it is that which has been handed down from saints and sages of the past, the embodiment of the unwritten law. So we read I 109: The Br. who departs from Ācāra does not attain the fruit of the Veda, but united to Ācāra he would become sharer in its full fruit. That is, the ordinances of Ācāra are placed on no lower level than the Veda itself as for as concerns its potency to give happiness hereafter — for this is ultimately what is intended by the «fruit of the Veda». The definition of Ācāra is given in the preceding çloka (quoted p. 4). It is that highest duty uttered in çruti: dharmaḥ çrutyuktaḥ and *smārta evaca*, that is, the ācāra rests no less on the utterances of the later sages (under smṛti the law books etc. are understood)[1]) who have preceded the time in which this was written than on that of the Veda itself. Ācāra is tapaso mūlam the root of ascetic (religious) fervour (110). So IV 178: The path on which his fathers and on which his fathers' fathers went — upon this path of the good let him also go and going upon this path he receives no injury.[2]) That the theory of Ācāra was subject to many exceptions in practice, as well as in āpat circumstances as in the number of unworthy representatives of the Br. caste, is shown below. But the theory, which was valid for every righteous Br., enslaved all action of the members of the Br. caste as of the other castes to the practices of the past. It is only when no precedent is at hand that he may follow his own desire — priyam ātmanaḥ. II 12. In this last quoted passage the Sadācāra is not reckoned as above as that delivered through çruti and smṛti, but as an independently received institution — perhaps retained through anecdotes and the like, and here, if we judge by the order of the words, the çruti and smṛti take precedence, but in all cases the private desire of the individual must recede before the practice which has been laid down for him aside from revelation and law in the example of the fathers — in Ācāra.

Better than the Br. is the parent. The ācārya is ten times better than the upādhyāya and the father an hundred times better than the ācārya. But the mother is a thousand times better than the father (gauraveṇa) II 145; but though the mother surpasses a thousand fathers, yet (II 225—26) the mother is the representative of the earth while the father is the representative of Prajāpati and the ācārya of Brahm (mūrti), moreover the elder brother is the manifestation or representative of Ātmā — therefore these are not to be despised by a Br. allthough he is oppressed (ārta) by them.

From the godlike or (perhaps a more correct expression) supernatural side of the Br.'s character we have now to examine his position where he is represented as having systematic and controlled relations with the other castes.

The six professional acts of the Br. have already been mentioned, repeated with scarcely a change, except in giving agrajanman as epithet equivalent to Br. in X 75, they are in (76) divided into three (sacrificing for others — teaching — and receiving gifts) which are called his jīvikā or means of livelihood, and (tacitly) three which are only of spiritual benefit, studying — giving sacrifices to the gods in his own behalf — and gifts to men. That the Br. was not always of the peaceful mode of life indicated by these statutes is sufficiently proved by reference to other literature. It remains to be seen if some reflex from this former period of more uncircumscribed life does not linger still in the Dh. Çās. of Manu. An allusion to the Brah. as soldier, that is as usurping the office of Ksh., is, I think, intimated by IV 167, which reads: ayudhyamānasya utpādya Brāhmaṇasya asṛgaṅgataḥ | duḥkhaṃ sumahad āpnoti pretya aprājñātayā naraḥ — whoever causes blood to flow from the limb of a Br. not actually engaged in battle. That we are to attribute this meaning to the root yudh as here used, is, I think, shown by its universal use to denote fighting in war.[1]) Cf. for instance such cases as VII 199 where the verb. med. is used in the same sense, or VII 200 etc. through this book. There is also a passage in the Mhbhā. through which, since the passage there given is evidently the same, we seem to have without doubt the meaning «in war» to supply here, for this occurs in the Mhbhā. text. I refer to XII 1224[2]) pragṛhya çastram āyāntam api vedāntagam raṇe jighāṃsantañ jighāmsīyān na tena Brahmahā bhavet. Here the word raṇe shows clearly that fighting in battle is meant and not perhaps an accidental scrimmage of personal character. This appears indeed to be an old formula; for we read in *Āpastamb. dha. sūtram*[3]) 1, 10. 29. 7. yo hiṃsārtham abhikrāntam hanti manyur eva manyum çpṛsati na tasmin dosha iti purāṇe, though we are here without special reference to war fighting (with the formula in Āp. Cf. Mbhā 1226 and 878 and Manu, VIII 350—351). This seems therefore through a negative condition to point to the fact that the actual occurrence was not unknown. Weber remarks in Ind. Stud. X 96 after quoting from Kauç. 93, 104: es gilt als unheilvoll wenn Br. die Waffen führen[4]) (*was also doch mehrfach vorkam.*)

In certain cases it is even enjoined upon the Br. to bear arms. The Br. must take arms (çastram dvijātibhir grāhyam where the Br. as dvija par excellence, as often, is to be understood, or at any rate included, if the expression is used generally) when law is threatened, and dvijātīnām varṇānāṃ viplave kālakārite — more over in his own defence and in a struggle for his rightful prerogatives (or gifts, Kull.: dakshiṇādhanagavādyapahāranimitte ca saṇgrāme) and to help a woman or a cow he is not in fault if he kill anyone VIII 348, 349.

The Br. may also change his mode of life in order to secure a support. For in IV 4. 5. 6 among the various permitted modes of life for a Br. are pramṛtam i. e. kar-

1) Ind. Stud. X s. 66. T. S. 2. 6. 10. 2 the penalty in M. IV 168. cf. M. XI 207.

2) Calcutta Edition.

3) Ed. Bühler.

4) And so acc. to Āp. 1. 10. 29. 6 even to take into the hand to look at., parīkshārtho'pi Br. āyuddhāni nādadhīta.

shaṇam or satyānṛtam, a very drastic equivalent for vāṇijyam. Kull. understands even kusīdam under this expression and quotes Gautama[1]) kṛshivāṇijye svayañcākṛte kusīdañca showing these apply to āpat cases, but they are not to be personally performed at other times. Kull. stands here on the standpoint of G.'s quotation, the latter's rule is not exclusive of anāpat (cf. K. to çl. 9). Acc. to Yāj. the Br. is simply directed to take to the profession of a Vaiç. in time of need, but to fling it by as soon as possible III 35. But Manu himself is more explicit. In X 81 occurs the rule: whenever the Br. cannot exist by his prescribed business then let him live by the regulations (modes of life) of a Ksh.; for that stands next to his own, and (82—83) when he can neither support himself as Br. nor as Ksh. then let him live kṛshigoraksham āsthāya i. e. as Vaiç. Let him however carefully keep away from kṛshi since it causes injury to those dependent on others.[2]) As a Vaiç., in trading, the Br. is, however, directed to be circumspect in the wares sold — viṭpaṇyam is allowed by the general permission, but he is not to sell human creatures — (thus otherwise permitted?) — he becomes a Çūdra in three days on selling milk, and other sales give him in seven nights the nature of a Vaiç. (86 flg.), but in general the Br. is directed to mind strictly his own business: yo anadhītya dvijo vedam anyatra kurate çramam sa jīvan eva çūdratvam .. gacchati. (Dvija = Br.) II 168. We have seen (above p. 9) that the Br. must logically be included under the head of those who are permitted in the list there given to have recourse even to

1) X 5. 6. K. to M. IV 6 (Calcutta. G. (Stenzler) «ca asvayaṇkṛte».

2) Cf. 84: Some say kṛshi is a good thing but, in reality it is not approved by the good, for the iron-mouthed piece of wood hurts the ground and its in-dwellers. 83, 84 and 85 are however as it seems to me a later addition. Kull. explains the contradiction between 82 and 83 by saying that goraksham must first be tried, and if this fail, kṛshi. But the contradiction in the text is hard to accept even in Manu, and the Ksh. appears rather suddenly here on the stage, wheras the sing. subj. is resumed again in 86. If the similar passage in Āpast. can have any influence here, we would notice that there is with him only one subject (Br.) avihitā Br. vanijyā padi vyavahareta paṇyānām apanyāṇi vyudasyan. I. 7. 20. 10 & 11.

servitude but that this is in IV 6 sharply forbidden as »çvavṛttiḥ». We may regard the latter perhaps as a later restriction. It is at least probably that Gautama, whose references to other lawgivers fall so generally together with those found even in the present metrical manavic text that they may be regarded as referring to the work presumably serving as a basis to our dhçās., in giving the direct reference (VII 23) to an authority holding a contrary opinion to his own, namely that a Çūd.'s mode of life may in extreme need be accepted by the Br., has reference to this point in (an earlier but) a similar version, and that this has been handed down preserved among the general clauses but denied when the point is especially brought into prominence. Such a procedure were not astonishing in M. Br. who follow the business of a servant are recognized and blamed in VIII 102.

Prof. Weber (Ind. Stud. X 40—41) gives a list of four privilegia and four duties which according to Çat. Br. 11. 5. 7. 1 are due the Br. and which the Br. should perform. The first are (arcā) reverence which is due him from every one, (dānam) gifts which one should give him, ajyeyatā his complete irrepressibility, avadhyatā (The-not-to-be-killed) his entire freedom from liability to a violent death or exemption from capital punishment. His four duties are (Brāhmaṇyam) a Br. lineage, (pratirūpacārya) a corresponding mode of life, (yaçaḥ) fame (through study of Veda etc.), (lokapakti) the teaching of the people.[1]) These I shall touch upon as occasion presents itself under the various paragraphs, without following at all the list as here given — at present in regard to the last mentioned of the Br. rights, his freedom from capital punishment, and what hangs together with this subject. The Br. is declared inviolable in body and his property cannot be confiscated. This is expressly stated in one or two çlokas quoted below, and therewith is the statement united that the Br. is also not to be corporally punished (akshata). That the opposite of this last passage is nevertheless logically inferable from the text of Manu I think can be shown to be the case. It seems to me the following passages show proof that the Br. is included among those liable to corporal punishment. I have shown above (p. 11) that the Br. is not excluded from the trials by fire, and if we take the text literally, that he must logically be included among those who are discussed in that passage, and that the restriction of particular punishments in this respect appears first by Yāj. A passage which under another head we shall have to quote again may be adduced here as a similar case where the Br. seems subject to corporal punishment. I refer to IX 235 in which the great criminals are discussed. The list evidently includes members of all castes — and so even K. since he explains the word surāpa as dvijātiḥ paishṭyāḥ pātā Br. ca paishṭīmādhvīgauḍīnām.

But now as to punishment. Here we can only through an evident misinterpretation exclude the Br., whom K. has here expressly mentioned, from the text. For in 236 we read, such among these four (sinners) as have not made the expiation the king should punish with a just corporal punishment as well as one of property. There is here no Br. mentioned; but according to 240 *all the castes* (sarve varṇāḥ) who have made expiation are not to be marked on the forehead (nāṇkyā . . lalāṭe syuḥ); but this expression unites the çloka with 237 where the branding is more particularly described, and this Kull. very rightly does. Closing with this we have the result that the Br. is to be corporally punished like the other castes. Nor can we exclude him on the strength of the following çlokas. For these çlokas give only the alternative mentioned in 240. If they have not performed a proper expiation the branding is to take place; but if the expiation has taken place they are not to be branded but to be fined the highest fine; the fine of the Br. is, however, (only) the middle one or he may be banished from the realm with all his possessions, but the others are to be either deprived of all their property or be banished [1]) acc. as the act is done with intention or not —

1) Pravāsanam is transl. by K. as if it could mean capital punishment but the opposition is plainly between the confiscation of property without banishment and confiscation with banishment added. Against the verbal translation of pravāsana with death is to remark that K. himself where he has no point to make, ex. gr. VII 124 translates with

such is the gist of 241—242. Not attempting to explain the alteration of punishment for the other castes I think it is still clear that the branding is enjoined as well for a Br. as for the others. It would be difficult to separate the çl. 241, with the reduction of the penalty for the Br., from 240. They express the case where the prāyaçcittam has been performed. But çl. 242 I should like to reject, since aside from this question it seems to be an illogical addition to the rules before given. We have had the fine for expiated crimes and the punishment for unexpiated, but if expiated the middle fine set in general is not explained, but contradicted, by resolving it into two possibilities kām° and akām° with respective punishments, so with unexpiated, or should this be additional to the branding? But this can only pass as a severer addition to kām°, why then akām° emphasized? The çl. seems to me either out of place or to be rejected. The point sought to be shown above however does not depend on its retention or rejection.

There is a passage in Yāj. which distinctly states that Br. are to be banished and branded, which seems scarcely possible to be true of Yāj. Dh. Çās. The çloka reads: A thief let the king kill with bodily injuries of various sorts, after he has restored what he has taken; but a Br. let him banish after branding him (sacihnam Br. kṛtvā) II 270. Are we to understand actual branding (so BR. and Stenzler) or merely putting a mark upon him i. e. distinctive dress or even public proclamation? I doubt if we can understand here such brand-marking as is elucidated in the above passage of M. but rather as in M. II 170 and in X 55 cihnay denotes no corporal punishment; so sacihna means «with a token or badge» of his crime, for instance shaving the head.

The ordinary punishment of the Br. however is, in case the crime is very severe, banishment; but the confiscation of the Br. property is not permitted VIII 380. The Br. must not be killed although he has committed the worst of crimes

deçānniḥsāraṇam — cf. the general use of the verb vas pra cf. VIII 123 pravāsayet = vivāsayet and ref. sub voc. in B. R. It seems impossible that it should mean death.

(sarvapāpeshu sthitaḥ) — He must be sent from the realm with all his property and unhurt, and, (381): No greater crime exists than that of killing a Br. The king must not even think of a Br.'s death (vadha); so VIII 123: The three lower castes let the king banish after bestowing punishment (daṇḍayitvā) but the Br. let him (only) banish. (cf. Y. II 81. 82) In the next (124) çloka we are still more positively told this; the places of bodily punishment are mentioned for the three castes, but akshato Br. vrajet. K. remarks to 123 that Govindarāja explains vivāsayet of the Br. by *nagnañ kuryāt* after levying the punishment, which from the foregoing çlokas is here one of money. Thereto Medhātithiḥ: Brāhmaṇasya vivāsastrvam vāṣopaharaṇañ gṛhabhañgo vā (iti ācashṭe), but vivāsayet is evidently the same as pravāsayet (banish) in the same line.[1])

1) Instead of capital punishment and apparently as an equivalent of what among other castes is prescribed as the death penalty we find in the case of the Br. the substitution of ignominious shaving of the head enjoined. This is not an unusual punishment among the Hindus and it must have been through an oversight that the author of *Indische Alterthumskunde* has denied this fact. The matter as an historical point is worth noticing; for on the basis of this denial Lassen has materially affected the reputation for veracity of a Greek writer on India. Lassen says namely Ind. Alt. Bd. III, 344—45 that among the principal reasons for rejecting the information given us by *Nikolaos of Damascus* is the incorrectness of his statements in regard to the punishments among the Hindus, for he says that those who had committed the heaviest crimes were obliged to let their hair be shaved off, since that was regarded as the most degrading punishment. To this Lassen remarks: «This law cannot pass as one taken from the information given by Megasthenes, nor as one really contained in the law-book of the Hindus; for cutting off the hair is not prescribed at all as a punishment in the Indian law-books and quite different penalties are enjoined for the worst crimes — ex. gr. the death of a Br.» (He then refers to Manu XII 54—72 flg. and Yāj. III 206 flg.) further «The idea that the deprivation of the hair of the head was regarded by the Indians as a disgrace may perhaps be one transferred to them from the Greeks, since it is also found in the Epos of Nonnos.» This whole paragraph rests on a false basis. A few extracts will show that Lassen had thought only of the threatened punishments of the next world and had not considered those of the practical life of the Hindus as given for instance in books VIII and XI. The quotation from M. XII 54—57

A very practical side of the Br.'s life meets us in the ordinance concerning fines and property of the Br. Though it cannot pertain to my object to discuss with any fulness the laws of taxation and exemption from money liabilities as they are laid down in the law book, yet the subject in so far as it appears to affect the relation of the Br. with the other castes cannot be left unnoticed. The right and duty of the Br. to receive gifts has already been noticed. It is the duty of men in general if not particularly forbidden to give the Br. wealth. One must give property acc. to XI 6 as much as possible to the wise Br. (viprāḥ). But though permitted he should not be over-desirous of obtaining wealth, for (IV 15): He (the Br.) should not see riches with eagerness nor obtain it by forbidden deeds, and neither when he has no money nor when he has money should he (receive it) from anyone at random (yatastataḥ).

Taxation of the Br., that is the wise Br., is absolutely forbidden VII 133. Though dying (with want, kshīṇadhano api Kull.) the king must not take a tax (kara) from a learned Br. nor should a Br. ever want for food in his realm; but the king (135) appointing him a proper support must protect him as a father does his own son (cf. pitṛvan nṛshu in VII 80). (Cf. Y. I 338, III 44). Not only the Çrotriya but even, VIII 394, a blind, lame, one nigh seventy years of age, and one

and Yāj. III 206 concerns the future where shaving the head is certainly not enjoined, but in this life the penalty is frequent enough. First of the Br. M. VIII 379. The punishment of the other castes may extend to death (prāṇāntika) but in the case of a Br. the expression daṇḍaḥ prāṇāntikaḥ means shaving the head (mauṇḍyam). That is: instead of the death penalty the shaving of the head must be substituted. Further, for a Kshatriya: VIII 375 (as expiation for a certain crime) «sahasram kshatriyo daṇḍyo, mauṇḍyam mūtreṇa ca arhati» even shaving with urine (K. kharamūtreṇa), and similarly VIII 384 mūtreṇa *mauṇḍyam* icchet tu Ksh. — It is also a part of the expiation in one of the penances for Br. murder XI 79 *kṛtavāpano* nivased grāmānte etc. Again, in XI 109, also in atoning (for upapātaka!), *kṛtavāpo* vased goshṭhe carmaṇā tena saṃvṛtaḥ — and finally even as a badge of disgrace for women it is prescribed: Yā tu kanyām prakuryāt *strī*, sā *sadyo* mauṇḍyam arhati — VIII 370. These quotations may release Nikolaos of Damascus from the suspicion that his account in regard to this point had no foundation in the Dharmaçāstram.

who performs service for a Çrotriya, should not pay the smallest tax. Under the last expression K. understands those who give money, corn, or service to a Çrotriya. Nor may certain Br. pay regular toll, VIII 407, Pravrajito muniḥ, Brāhmaṇā liñginaçca eva na dāpyās tārikam tare. The Br. receive the property if there fail the sapiṇḍa the sakulya ācārya and çishya — such Br. as are veda-wise, pure, with subdued passions (or generous, dānta) IX 188. Property which the wise Br. finds and which has formerly been hidden he may take complete possession of since, he is lord of all, VIII 37. That is: he need not give up the usual tribute of a sixth.[1])

The Br. is regarded as a thief if he take property (either through sacrificing or teaching) from the hand of one who has taken that which has not been given — yathā stenas tathā saḥ VIII 340.[2]) The property which the Br. obtains by a forbidden act must be given up, and the sin atoned for with prayer and penance — so property received from a wicked man XI 194. 195 and flg.

The wealth of the mahāpātakinaḥ is when confiscated either flung into the water or given to a Br., since Varuṇa is the īço daṇḍasya and the Br. is īçaḥ sarvasya jagataḥ IX 243—245. The property of a Br. is not lost as is that of other men (excepting that of the king) by the law of ten years use by others (explained in VIII 147). Na(çrotriyasvam) bhogena pranaçyati VIII 149. The king may under no circumstances take a Br.'s property; but if there are no heirs the king may take the property of the other castes IX 189, (regarding inheritance).

I close this paragraph with such general regulations con-

1) Kull. quotes Yāj. II 34—35, M. I 100, and Nārada, to show this pertains to all the Br. has found, and stigmatizes the opposed opinion of Medhātithi and Govindarāja as «anārsham» styling the same «svakalpitam» — but pūrvopanihitam must be a restriction and the point seems well taken by G. and M.

2) Kull. gives the certainly sensible, but from the standpoint of his Brahmanhood somewhat remarkable, addition (cauratulyo jñeyaḥ) ataḥ sa iva daṇḍyaḥ — which would commit him to capital punishment, or at least loss of a limb.

cerning the Br. as may touch upon his other relations with the lower castes.

The Br. is responsible for his pupil, VIII 317. The fault of the scholar and sacrificer belongs to the Guru — as a thief's belongs to the king. From 316 the meaning is if the king do not punish the thief, so with the student (if unpunished?), but with the yājya (?) — (Kull. yājyaçca — — yājake *kshamamāṇe* pāpam nikshipati).

A Br. who is unhonoured as a guest takes on the other hand all the good of one who even lives by gleaning and has made offerings by the five fires — III 100 (cf. IV 4. 5. 9). The Br. addresses the elder with the word «it is I» — giving his name II 122 (130), so with ṛtvij, guru, addressing them though younger in the same way.

The priest is held strictly to his agreements. If a priest (ṛtvij) leave his work at a sacrifice, his share shall only be according to his work with the other sacrificers, and if the dakshiṇāḥ are already given and he then desert his work, he shall receive his full share, but he must cause some one else to complete his work for him VIII 206—207 and VIII 388. The yājya who forsakes the ṛtvij and the ṛtvij who forsakes the yājya are to be fined 100 (paṇas) provided they be sinless and capable (of doing their respective work).

Only one who has read all the Vedas (pāraga) may be a hotar; a girl, a young woman, a fool, a sick man, and an uninvested one may not be hotā — — agnihotrasya XI 36. 37.

Three things have the gods ordained as pure for a Br., that which is sprinkled with water, that which is unseen, and that which is praised with the voice V 127. — Some things are always pure — the hand of a workman, the mouth of a woman etc. (129—130).

The lightness with which the expression degrading to a mixed class etc. is used is shown by XI 69—70 and elsewhere. Killing an ass, horse, snake, sheep etc.[1]), çūdrasevanam, vāṇijyam, and receiving gifts from the unworthy, render one unworthy to receive gifts. The Br. sinks acc.

to XI 98 to the state of a Çūdra if the holiness received into his body (kāyagatam Brahma) is stained with intoxicating drink. (v. p. 19). The Br., if we are to credit Kull.'s explanation, is once presented us in the light of a sorcerer or as granting through magical powers the desires of bad men. The text however is very simple, namely in IX 268 among the methods given for catching thieves by experts is given the following, Brāhmaṇānām darçanaiḥ, and this is interpreted by the Commentator as follows. The expert goes to the thieves and says to them «There is a certain Br., he understands how to enable us to procure the money we wish to obtain, let us interview him» — which would presuppose perhaps the use of a sort of A. V. song — for though not accepted by M. as a Veda the A. V. collection is nevertheless not unknown.

The Vipra is purified if he kill all the worlds and receives gifts from anyone, if he only remember the Ṛgveda, and on repeating the saṃhitā of any of the three Vedas three times he is released from all sin XI 262—263 (cf. 259).

All sin sinks out of sight in the Veda, yathā mahāhradam prāpya kshiptam loshṭam vinaçyati (264). The extinction of all crimes declared in these çlokas and in 247 flg. would lead us to suppose that this passage is of later date than the mass of the work, or that the feat of remembering the whole Veda, or even the Ṛk, and the other necessary attainments for this universal absolution were not of very frequent occurence. As a matter of legal fact, in the face of the many minute laws such rules as these would nullify, they deserve no serious attention.

Denial of Brahmanhood is finable — He who denies the learning, the country, the class, or the (karmaçārīram)[1]) saṃskāra (of a Br.), through insolence, shall be fined 200 (paṇas). VIII 273. K. This means for one of the same caste v. 276. The Br.'s position as dependent on the three states of rāja — tamas — and sattva is declared in XII 48. 49. In the

1) Karmaçārīram might be taken in opposition to kāṇa — khañja of 274. His ability to perform bodily functions (?).

rank prathamā sāttvikī gatiḥ belong devotees, ascetics and priests, in the dvitīyā sāttv. gat. are yajvānaḥ and ṛshayaḥ.[1])

IIIb. Br. and Br.

The Relations of Br. to Br. meet us in the main when we inspect the religious side of his character — the social and legal side shows also however a tendency to distinguish sharply between those Br. who are to be held worthy of honour, and those on the other hand who are through neglect of duties to be despised. The main point in which the Br. is to observe the greatest care with his brother Br. is in the reception of gifts at a çrāddha. Weber (Ind. Stud. X s. 46) has already remarked that the injunctions in regard to the reception of guests at a pitryam or daivam (karma) are contradictory to the sentiment expressed in III 149 «Let the Br. not examine (Na parīksheta) a Br. at a daivaṃ karma but at a pitryaṃ karma let him examine the Br. with great care».

Weber does not accept (since he does not notice it) the precise remark of Kull. that parīksheta means «Examine into his descent — his ancestry». This meaning which seems to accord well with the fact that the feast where the examination is to be held is one to the ancestors would remove the direct opposition in 149 to the extended directions following, which are concerned with the moral character and manner of life and are valid for both çrāddha. Judging from the list of those forbidden to be present we find a quantity of irregularities which must have prevailed at that time. Among others in III 164 the gaṇānām (eva) yājakaḥ — sacrificer to the legions (gods) (usually of Çiva's escort [later] P. W.) — (vināyaka [Gaṇeça] ādigaṇayāgakṛt. Kull.) also (152) vṛshalavṛtiḥ — and (155) vṛshalīpatiḥ husband of a vṛshala woman, (153) usurer, (154) paçupāla, (156), a priest who teaches the Veda for money (bhṛtakādhyāpaka) and he who employs such a teacher (bhṛtakādhyāpita), a Çūdra's pupil and his Guru — (cf. Yāj. I 223), (162) yuddhācāryaḥ, (165) kṛshijīva, (158) sailor and Vandin. Unworthy of either havya (offerings to gods) or kavya (to manes) are the viprāḥ who are thieves, fallen, eunuchs, atheists (150) (Y. I 224). — These (167) are excluded as unworthy Brs. etān vigarhitācārān apāṅkteyān dvijādhamān ubhayatra (i. e. from daivaṃ karma and pitryaṃ karma) vivarjayet.[1])

The broken pieces which fall on the ground are received by the deceased asaṃskṛtā Br. III 245.

On the day before the feast or on the same day he should invite at least three priests of the right sort (nimantrayeta trayavarān saṃyagviprān yathoditān III 187 one Br. should be invited to pitryam, but none to the vaiçvadevaçrāddha III 83. At pitryam three guests, and at daivam two, or one in each. III 125.

He must examine throughly (in regard to his lineage K.) a Br. who has read the whole Veda. Such an one is worthy of the gift of havya and kavya, he is called a guest. III 130. The stress is here laid on vedapāraga: such an one he must examine, cf. 128. The four kinds of Br. are the jñānanishṭha, those devoted to knowledge, the taponishṭha, exercising ascetic penance, tapaḥsvādhyāyānishṭha, devoted to ascetic exercises and study, and those devoted to sacrifice, karmanishṭha. Among these the kavya should be placed before the first, the havya offerings before all four III 134 —135.[2])

Food should be given to those who have devoted themselves to one branch of vedic study III 145. Kavya and havya bring great reward if given to a learned priest, the most worthy vipra III 128. And among the paṇktipāvanāḥ or purifiers of the company are triṇāciketaḥ, pañcāgniḥ, trisuparṇaḥ, shaḍaṅgavid, brāhmyadeyātmasantānaḥ, the best sāma-reader, one who knows the meaning of the Veda

1) The Vandin or Bandin (of 158) if included in etān must be taken generally as hired singer. It is properly one of the lowest of the mixed castes v. X 48 where Kull. quotes from Baudhāyana that the Madgu (mentioned but not explained by Manu) is the son of a Br. on Vandistrī, and Kull. himself explains Vandistrī as bandhistrī or offspring of the Ksh. on a Çūdrā — thus equals Ugrā —.

2) The division is similar to the three kinds of snātaka, vidyāsn°, vratasn° & vidyāvratasna° K. to III 2. (Hārīta) cf. Stenzler's note to Açv. Gṛh. sūt. I 22. 3.

and one who teaches it, and a Brahmacārin (sahasradaḥ), and one an hundred years old. III 185.

One should not at a çrāddha feed a friend, but feed the dvija who is neither friend nor foe III 138. At pleasure let him honour a friend at a çrāddha (!) but not a foe, since food eaten by an enemy is useless for the next life III 144. Food at çrāddha given to a soma-seller, physician, usurer, trader, is useless here and hereafter — and to a paunarbhavaḥ (dvijaḥ) is like an offering on ashes III 180, 181 — of priests in this guise.

From this list of forbidden Br. one sees plainly that the rules of the sacred order were broken in all directions. It is scarcely possible that such a minute and exhaustive grouping of Brahmanic delinquents had been inserted in the law, were the subjects treated of a list of imaginative criminals. Aside from crimes against morality which such degenerate priests are here represented as committing, we have the laws of professional life broken, irreligion, and disbelief in the recognized deities, the worst rejection of the caste laws, and an unlawful use of priestly learning. From the description of the different modes of life of those Br. worthy of honour, we see that the Br. were accustomed to follow some one branch of study to the exclusion of other branches, that some of these branches were reckoned higher than others, that the permission of giving a Br. the full rights of his caste was only conceded upon a careful inspection of either his character or his birth, and from this we draw the conclusion that the fact that a man was member of the Brahmanic order was in no way sufficient to preclude the possibility of his being looked upon with a varying amount of respect, or, in other words, it was not absolutely the highest to be a Brahman, but that members of the Brahmanic caste were strictly subservient to an unconditionally necessary rule of conduct and that resting on this alone the Br. was entitled to respect or regard.

Apart from the consideration of those breaking or keeping the ruler of their caste, we have, inside the bound of worthy caste members, only a distinction in pursuit of study or discipline, a preference for Br. who come from one part of India,[1]) and the artificial preference given out of purely practical grounds to those occupying the second stadium in the regular course of Br. life. The four stages need not be described, sufficient to illustrate this is VI 89: of all these (i. e. the Brahmacārin, gṛhastha, vānaprastha, yati, v. 87) according to the ordinances of Veda and Smṛti, the gṛhastha is declared to be the best; for he supports the other three orders. So in III 77—78 where the dependence of the other āçramāḥ on the gṛhastha is represented as that of all animate nature on the breath of life (vāyu K. prāṇākhyo vāyu) since the other three classes are dependent on the gṛhastha for food and knowledge — tasmāj jyeshṭhāçramo gṛhī.

A curious comparison in the third book informs us that it is better for the Br. to have a father who has read the Vedas than to have read them himself. If one's father is unlearned but the son is learned in the Vedas, or the son being unlearned and the father learned in the Vedas, then he is the better whose father is learned, but the other is to be honoured in honouring the mantras.[2]) III 136. 137.

We may add to the differences made between the virtuous that of IV 7. 8. The best Br. is he who does not store up for the morrow (he may have a large store, a smaller store, enough for three days, or none for the morrow) — he has through his virtue best conquered the world.

As we saw that Br. are to be honoured according as they are true to their prescribed duty or not, so we find that the gifts given to the Br. produce unequal results just as the receivers are worthy of much or little honour. VII 85: A gift to one not a Br. (Ksh. etc. Kull.) is of

1) II 18—20 v. p. 4.

2) Acc. to K. the putra is here the Br. himself. It is better that the father be learned than that the man himself be learned — it is better, however, it seems to me, if we regard three generations as represented here and the sense were that the Br. who has a learned father is worthy of more honour than he who has a learned son. The rel. yasya in first çloka (a) is to be supplied with putra in (b). Such a row is presented in Çat. Br. 14. 9. 4. 29. though the connection is not the same (quoted Ind. Stud. X 120).

middle virtue (samam dānam) (K. samaphalam), twofold, however, to one who calls himself a Br., to a learned Br. an hundred thousand fold, but to one who has studied all the Vedas, infinite (cf. çl. 83). So III 142: As a sower takes no fruit if he sow his seed in poor soil, so giving havis to a Br. who does not know the Veda the giver receives no fruit.

Dependent on the learning of the Br. is the virtue of the offering as represented in III 97 — Havya and kavya amount to nothing if they are given to ignorant priests (vipra) (these are stigmatized as priests whose being is ashes — bhasmībhūta) (cf. III 179), add in this connection IV 199. Those who commit a crime and perform a penance, under pretence of virtue, covering up the evil with the penance (varta — vow of penance), for the sake of deceiving women and Çūdras, are, when they are dead, despised by the declarers of the Veda, and (II 157) like an elephant made of a block of wood, like deer made of leather, so is a Br. who has not recited the holy texts — they are mere names. [1]) As the Br. is distinguished above all other created things (I 96. p. 24) so the verse following this comparison presents the difference between the Br. themselves: Best among the Br. are the wise, best among the wise are those who have firm characters, among those with firm characters the best are those who are active, among the active those who are learned in the Vedas (or are acquainted with the divinity) I 97. In Yāj. I 199 we have also a distinction made between the Br.: those who sacrifice are better than those who study the Veda, and better than these those who know the adhyātma, so M. XII 85 ātmajñānam param smṛtam. And yet we find the unearthly holiness given by the study of the Veda is denied and the law asserts the superiority of morality over religious knowledge without morality (II 118). The Br. who acts in accordance with temperance (suyantritaḥ is evidently of controlled well regulated character, but Kull. çāstraniyamitaḥ) is, although he can repeat nothing

1) Cf. Mbhā. XII 1338 and in 1340 the comparison is extended: like a bird without its wing, a village without corn, or a well without water.

more than the sāvitrī, yet better than he who eats every thing, sells every thing, and who is of uncontrolled disposition, although he has learned the three Vedas. Were Kull.'s explanation correct it would evince a greater reverence for smṛti than for çruti. We may add here IV 176 (The Br. must avoid exercising) even his right if it be accompanied by unpleasant consequences and is *disapproved by the world;* in which the sentiment of the world is placed antagonistic to, and indeed prevailing over, his right, which stands in a measure as representative of the çruti law. But perhaps «asukhodarka» may be the strong point in this concession.

The intercourse of Br. with Br. is founded on ceremonial restrictions. Āyushmān bhava «Saumya» iti vācyo vipro abhivādane. We have then a grammatical note which is without parallel in Manu, ăkāraçca asya nāmno ante vācyaḥ pūrvāksharaḥ plutaḥ — This is the rule given in II 125. In the next çloka Manu says that the vipra who does not know the response to a salutation must not be addressed by a wise man, yathā çūdras tathaiva saḥ.[1])

The Br. is bound to observe social duties: The priest who does not invite his next neighbour, and the one next to this one when he gives a feast for twenty twice born, provided they be worthy, is fined a māshaka VIII 392 cf. Yāj. II 263 «ten paṇas». Also in the following: A Çrotriya not inviting another good Çrotriya at a bhūtikarma (kṛtyam) (K. vivāhādishu) shall pay twice as much as the feast cost (tadannan dviguṇan dāpyaḥ) and a gold māshaka (K. limits very reasonably to those of the previous çloka).

The intercourse of the Br. is directed to be only with the highest, by neglect of this he descends to Çūdra-ship. IV 245. He is however to seek disrespect as if it were honey, II 162.

A formula, twice given with slightly varying words, gives the Br. the right to beat no one except a son and a pupil and these for the sake of correction IV 164. But (with

1) Kull. notes that this is only applicable to the Br. The syllable is not pluta in the case of Ksh. and Vaiç. (Kātyāyana), nor of a Çūdra (Pāṇ), nor of a woman (Kātyāyana).

extended privilege) in VIII 299, he may besides these beat his wife, own brother, and slave. These are to be beaten with a rope or stick if they have done wrong. (Since the slave is included the addition is noteworthy: pṛshṭhatas tu, çarīrasya na uttamāñge kathañcana.) Cf. Yāj. I 155 putram çishyañ ca tāḍayet.

The ācārya, teacher (pravaktar), father, mother, and Guru, one should not injure; so also in general, Brahmans, cows, and all those who practice austerities, IV 162. In the distribution at a sacrifice the Adhvaryu should take the chariot (ratha), and the Brahmā the horse, or the Hotar the horse, and the Udgātar, the waggon (anas) VIII 209 in regard to the pratyañgadakshiṇāḥ of 207. In the distribution among the priests, the first four (of 16) have half the dakshiṇāḥ, the next four the half of that, the third four have a third, and the fourth four have a fourth (210).[1]

A year's severe penance (kṛcchrābdena) is the purification prescribed the Br. who steals intentionally grain food or money from the house of a man of the same caste XI 163.

From these general notes of Br. relations within the caste boundary, we pass rather to the most important point of contact between Br. and Br., and this in found in the right which the Br. as a body possesses over the individual members of the caste, in respect to exclusion from, and reinstatement in, the rights of their order, and in the power which is permitted the Br. caste of prescribing law in cases left unsettled by the Dh.çāst. The term degraded, or fallen (patita), is, however lightly used at times as a threat, not without legal as well as moral importance. The patita is indeed, till the atonement of the sin has taken place, deprived of civil rights, and the rite by which he recovers possession of these lost rights is therefore not without importance. From XI 183—185 we learn that the water offering is to be made in the case of a patita (Kull. mahāpātakin, which is a limitation unwarranted by the text) and the ceremony, together with the impurity thereby brought

1) The arithmetic of the text is false but cf. Kātyāyana (Kull.).

upon the relations, is as if the patita were dead (pretavat), that is, he practically has ceased to exist for his family, and in consequence intercourse with him must cease, and he is deprived of the right of inheriting property, together with the loss of jyeshṭhatā, of those privileges which he should have were he the eldest in the family. This is in Yāj. (III 295) not so explicitly stated: we are there told (the svabāndhavāḥ) vahiḥ kuryuḥ *sarvakāryeshu* ca eva tam. If however the text of Manu is to be construed literally we have the sinner (of undetermined caste) absolutely nullified as a political or legal figure, until after the proper performance of the prāyaçcittam.

We learn moreover (and here the case is for the Br. alone) in the çlokas following, XI 196. 197, that this fallen man who has performed the penance) the sin of taking a gift from a bad man is here the case handled) is by this penance purified as far as his conscience goes. The penance however does not put him back again on the level he has lost *without the concurrence of other Br.* and it is this formal recognition by the Br. of his purification which must give or reject his re-admission to his own privileges. (After the penance) returning thin with fasting from the cow-pasture, (place of penance v. 195), the Br. should address him as he makes obeisance to them (saying): wilt thou, O dear one, have equality (again with us) (196), upon his saying «satyam» let them receive him upon the spot occupied by the cows. The reception of the Br. is here regarded as a necessary adjunct to his purification and re-admission to caste rights, and if such is the case, the Br. must have been in great measure dependent on the goodwill and readiness of the other Br. to accede to his return. What this company of Br. was we have now to investigate; the statements in Manu on this point are few and scattered. It appears, by uniting these statements, that this is the same body who are to declare prāyaçcittam where no decision has been given by the regular law. In regard to such a body we have in XI 210 the statement: For the releasing 'from crimes the expiation of which has not been declared, after considering the crime and the ability (of the criminal to perform the penance) let — establish the penalty (prāyaçcittam.) What are we to supply as the subject of the verb (prakalpayet)? Sir W^m. Jones gives «the Assembly» which is neither in the text, nor to be extracted from the immediate context, nor given by Kull. We are presumably to connect this power which regulates these laws with the Br. mentioned above in 196, 197, but that is an arrangement only spoken of for Br. whereas this at least in its general language, and, from a word of K.'s in explanation, would seem to have more general functions, for K. in explaining pāpānām says pratilomajavadhādikṛtānām, but this implies that the laws were relative to the lower castes also, for a Br. cannot commit vadha pratilo° ; also Y. III 294 leaves the matter in doubt, since he says, prāyaçcittam prakalpyam syād yatra ca uktā na nishkṛtiḥ — (Stenzler: «soll *man* bestimmen») We can scarcely unite the subj. with that of the verse preceding, giving the same government to prakalpayet as to caret and kurvīta; for the permission not of selecting, but of creating a penance, is one not constituted through Manu's injunctions elsewhere. But we find the assembly, that is the parishad, elsewhere called upon to exercise this function, which may give us the right to supply the same as subj. here. In 227 of same book we have one more indefinite clause like the one quoted «The twice born may be purified by these laws when their guilt is known, but otherwise — — «mantrair homaiçca çodhayet» — here the subject is also not clear, Kull. however mentions the purification as performed by the parishad.[1]) Cf. Y. III 301. The position of the Br. in this respect is yet more distinctly stated in çl. 86. Even three wise Br. shall declare expiation — — the word of the wise is a means of purification. In 83 we are also told that a Br. (killing accidentally another Br.) is released by stating his crime in the presence of the lords of earth and the lords of men, etc. The Ksh. form a factor here not mentioned in the other cases and settles this case as not being an example of the parishad, but simply an assembly about an açva (haya) medha sacrifice. If we are entitled to distin-

1) In XI 193 (192) ādiçet lacks a subject in the same way.

guish between the religious and civil side of this parishad's prerogatives, we shall have to class these cases among the first. It remains to be seen if we have any ground for the latter branch. The parishad is of course to be distinguished from the sabhā of book VIII, for the latter is in conjunction with the king, has only the function of explaining laws, not of making them, and consists acc. to Bṛhasp. (Mitāksh. to Y. II 2) of at most seven members. For the possibly legal side of the functions to be exercised by the parishad we have only one passage in Manu. Anāmnāteshu dharmeshu — — yaṃ çishṭā brāhmaṇā brūyuḥ sa dharmaḥ syād — — these are required to be men well acquainted with the sacred works — what ever dharma the parishad of at least ten or at least three virtuous men shall constitute, this it shall not allow to be changed.[1]) These men shall consist of those learned in Vedas, haituka, tarkin etc., but if only three they shall know respectively the Ṛg., Yāj. and Sāmavedas. Even one may decide the law if he be vedavid[2]) XII 108 to 113 (cf. Y. I 9), and (114): A parishad is not constituted by an assembly of a thousand Br., if they have not performed the proper rites and are ignorant of Veda, subsisting only by the name of their caste. According to the passage in Mbhā. just referred to, which runs quite parallel to this, the case is one dharmasaṃçaye . i. e. when there is a doubt in the case, and here where the points of duty are anāmnāta or not explained in the regular Dh. Çāstra. In the cases first mentioned we were confined to the adjustment of prāyaç-cittam, or duties connected with the fulfilment of the same, but the word dharma seems to imply a wider scope. The stress laid on the çāstra which they are to learn, seems to give this parishad the adjustment of legal rights on all points of law left unexplained; but dharma can mean as well points of duty in regard to state, as in regard to personal duties, or simple decisions in regard to right and wrong action. It is however not to be thought of that the Br. should in

1) Mbhā. XII 1312.

2) Vedavid! K. remarks that Veda means here smṛti as well as çruti.

general regulate or create laws or settle legal points on their own responsibility, and in this case the king is not included. It is however possible that the Br. was to exercise this privilege inside the circle of his caste, and thus these words would apply to the adjustment of legal rights and duties for future cases as well as present. If the Mbhā. quotation were allowed to influence the manavic text we should have a simple function of the sabhā elucidated; but here it is not in a perplexity between different laws, but where there are no laws to construct them, which is giving a widely extended legislative power. If we include under dharma such cases as these, we have two distinct sides to the parishad, if however dharma is to represent only religious duties etc., then it is scarcely to be distinguished in the XIIth from the company arranging prāyaçcittam in the XIth. Dharma seems to me however to be used in a wider sense than this.[1])

1) The parishad of Manu is not farther described. There is however a passage in Y. which may merit examination in this connection. In the çlokas from this Dh.çās. quoted above (I 9 and III 301) contain the only direct references in regard to the parishad (parshad) from Y. Dhç. In I 9 however it is identified with traividyam (catvāro vedadharmajñāḥ parshat traividyam eva vā). The traividyam is described in the second book of Yāj. from 185 flg. The king must erect in the city a building where he settles Br. — the Traividyam (Stenzler: «als vedakundige Körperschaft») — whom he supplies with the necessities of life and addresses with the words «Your duty should be carefully observed». Whatever right (or duty) of the assembly (sāmayiko dharmaḥ) does not conflict with the private duty (of a member), and whatever duty is enjoined upon them by the king, this must be observed by them. Who ever appropriates the common property of the assembly (gaṇadravyam) or disregards an agreement shall be deprived of his whole property and be banished. The word of those who speak for the good of the assembly (samūha) shall be executed by all; who ever speaks otherwise shall be fined the first fine . . . after honouring them . . . the king shall dismiss those who have come on business of the samūha — that which one as agent of the samūha receives he must deliver up or be fined. This is also the rule for çreṇi, naigama, pāshaṇḍi (!) and gaṇa (185—192). In spite of the fact that this traividyam is identified by Y. in I 9 with parishad (and this is perhaps even manavic if we consider the words traividyo and parishad standing the one as epithet of the other in XII 111) we yet see that there is no recognition of such a parishad as this in Manu, for the function of the manavic

IIIc. We have now to treat of the specific relations of the Br. with the under castes, excluding for the present those with the Ksh. which are separately treated. Some repetitions between the above paragraphs and this may be unavoidable, but the object of this section is to exhibit the direct contact of the Br. with the lower castes, while we have given above only the universal statutes for the castes in general.

I have already noted some general restrictions in regard to the principal point in which the daily intercourse of the Br. with the under castes is presented us, namely that of accepting gifts (v. p. 33). Parallel to IV 15, quoted above, we have a more positive restriction in this particular: Al-

parishad of the eleventh book differs materially, and in fact the arrangement here depicted constitutes essentially a business corporation which has its own business transactions, is founded on a common money fund and is in some measure controlled and appearantly directed by the king (dharmo rājakṛtaḥ 186); moreover it is identical in restriction and rights with the corporations of the other castes and is even termed a samūha the general designation for a business union. From this I think we may draw the conclusion that the traividyam of Yāj. was nothing more than one of the business classes an earlier stage of whose development we find in Manu VIII 211 and 221 without description, the general rules for the conduct of samūha of all kinds being here propounded. The assembly must, however, unless Y. uses the words in different senses, have had at least religious jurisdiction in some points, as we have seen from III 301, and that the corporations in general acc. to Y. had a certain power we learn from II 30, for understanding under pūgāḥ and çreṇayaḥ business unions, we are told that these were next important to the king's judges in deciding law cases; but it is uncertain whether we are to take this as presenting an active power in giving decisions, or only as furnishing through their customs precedents for the courts to act upon. The samūha of Br. in Manu is nothing more than a row of priests who perform a sacrifice together and divide among themselves the dakshiṇāḥ, wheras the parishad as we have seen had functions entitling them to regulate dharma. As we see in Yāj. the parshad is as traividyam in IInd bk. concerned with business, but in IIIrd book is simply for the purpose of settling prāyaçcitam; so we may perhaps accept as forerunner the division in Manu of a parshad on the one hand secular in its duties on the other religious. The decisions of the assembly of Manu appear to be final and independent.

though the Br. has a right to receive gifts (in any instance) yet let him avoid the inclination to do so,[1]) for by receiving gifts his glory departs from him. IV 186 so Y. I 213. He who accepts not a gift when he has a right to receive it attains the blooming world of the generous. Following the passages in which complete freedom of the Br. in regard to changing his mode of life in times of need is inculcated, we have a permission of like nature for the pratigraha; a permission which annihilates the strict law of receiving gifts as thoroughly as the other did away with the regulation of his mode of life in āpat cases, for we are told the Br. may if hungry accept of anyone. X 101 flg. In case the Br. though in distress for subsistence will not become a Ksh. or Vaiç. he may receive gifts from anyone (sarvataḥ); for neither from teaching the Veda, nor (general) sacrifice, nor from (ordinarily) contemned acception of gifts is there any fault on the part of the Br.; for he is like water and fire (cf. Y. III 41) and he who takes food when in danger of death (starvation) from anyone (yatastataḥ) is soiled as little thereby as the atmosphere is by mud (101. 104); he may (112) also glean from anyone ears or grains of corn. Compare with this XI 16: A Br. if hungry after long fasting may take gifts even from a wrong doer (Kull. thief and the like) and following in X 109—111: If one considers the three sins of receiving gifts, sacrificing, or teaching (indiscriminately, or for money?), the reception of gifts appears the worst, because the first two can only be done for those initiated (with the saṃskāra) whereas one may take gifts even from a Çūdra [2]) or the lowest men — the first are further described as expiable by sacrifice and prayer; the last only by severe

1) Prasangaṃ tatra varjayet P. W. translates «Er vermeide das Eintreten dieses Falles» but the same word is employed in the same connection in çl. 15. where the meaning of desire or inclination seems necessary.

2) A delicate distinction in IV 223 permits the Br. to take food which is raw, but not food which is cooked, from a Çūdra, if in need. Acc. to XI 16 he must wait till the seventh meal and then take from any one who does not perform sacrifices, but he must explain why to the owner — T. S. 2. 2. 6. 2. (Ind. St. X 58).

penance (tapasā). Between these sets of quotations in X[th] book is slipped in a list of Br. who in need received food from base men — Ajīgarta, Viçvāmitra etc.

Contradictions from these passages in book X lie on the surface. We are told in one breath that the Br. may accept from any one if in peril of his life, or he may sacrifice or teach (for the upper castes), and we are immediately afterwards informed that the Br. must do penance under any circumstances; for such a breach of right conduct and the reception of gifts (from unworthy persons) is particularly to be atoned for with severe penance although we have just learned that the Br. cannot become impure by such a sin.

We meet then the same principle at work in this case which we have found in the change of profession, that, namely, the forbidden contact of the Br. with the under caste is not of such character that it should prevent his making use of this caste when his life is in peril. It is no point of a creed to be maintained at any costs. The sanctity of the Br. may be contaminated by the lowest men if there is need. The plea that the Br. holiness is so great that it cannot be sullied is nullified by the fact that it is sullied on all other occasions and the sin must be atoned for. The number of sages who are here brought forward only show that the Br. desires to excuse that which he feels to be inconsistent with his teachings, but which is thus ipso facto proved as of less importance than that he should support his abhorrence of the act by his life.[1])

The reception of gifts, or taking of goods, may be either for the private good of the Br. or for the purpose of sacrifice. The Br. in the latter case may take one needed requisite from the house of a Vaiçya who has much cattle but does not perform his religious duties and does not drink the soma, or three, or two, from the house of a Çūdra (Na hi çūdrasya yajñeshu kaçcid asti pratigrahaḥ) even kuṭumbābhyām (K. translates as meaning Br. or Ksh.) and also

1) We may perhaps regard the second clause as a later addition (111) or take it as a general amplification — but we are entitled to supply the limitation of āpadi as well here as in the preceding.

from (a Br.) who does not give but accepts gifts XI 12—15 (K. adds balena cauryena vā haret). 20. Āsurasvam is the wealth of those who do not sacrifice, against the devasvam, property of the righteous (K. āsur° can be carried off for sacrificial purposes). But the Br. must not beg (bhikshetu) any thing from a Çūd. for sacrifice, or he becomes a Caṇḍāla after death XI 24; so Y. I 127. K. observes that he can *take* but not beg from a Çūd. (13). Perfect liberty is thus granted to take from the under castes for the purpose of a sacrifice. In accepting gifts for his own benefit except in cases of need, as seen above, the Br. is much restricted. He may always take however from a good man when desirous of support if his Gurus (parents) are dead, or he dwells apart from them, IV 252 and 247. 248. The Br. may receive wood, water, roots, fruit, food, and what is given unasked, from every one; so honey, and release from danger, even from a dushkṛtakarman may he take alms (bhikshā), v. Y. I 215, K. Exceptions in 213 etc. Cf. IV 250 articles he should not reject.[1]) In IV 251 the two are united; for the sake of honouring guests, guru, gods, he should take from any one but Na tu tṛpyet svayan tataḥ. He must not eat the food of a singer, carpenter, usurer (so Vaiçya cf. Āpast. 1. 6. 18. 22 and broader in 9) a consecrated person, nor of a Çūdra, nor of a physician, nor hunter, nor town food, nor of fallen men, nor of a dancer, nor of one who sells a ceremony (kratuvikrayiṇaḥ), nor of a tailor, smith, nishāda, actor, goldmaker, veṇa, an armour maker, dog-owner, washerman, nor dyer IV 210 to 218 other designations irrelative to caste are omitted[2]) (cf. Mbhā XII 1322 etc.). The loose arrangement of the work is well shown in this passage — there follows after this list the statement that king's food takes away his glory, and so with others mentioned in the list.

1) Acc. to Āpast. he may eat the food of any one of the castes except Çūdra (iti eke but) even of him if he be entirely devoted to his duty (or his private servant, dharmopanata) I 6. 18. 13 and 14.

2) To IV 251 cf. Āpast. sarvadā çūdrata ugrato vā ācāryārthasyāharaṇam dhārmyam iti eke; but Āp. himself gives as condition vishamagate — — ācārye Āp. 1. 2. 7. 21 and 20. This is for the vedadakshiṇā on ending his studies, kṛtvā vidyām (19).

Exactly rājā however is not in the list at all, the adjustment of this matter being together with gifts settled in IV 33, 83 and in bks. VIII and X.

The especial mention of the usurer may perhaps indicate that the Vaiçya's employments were not all regarded in the same light. Already (in X 84) we have seen that the shepherd life was preferred for the Br. to the agricultural. The mode of life of the Vaiçya would thus be approved according to its chronological development, as we can practically trace it in the earlier literature: first nomadic, and then as a member of a settled folk the agricultural, finally with the development of trade the lending of money with its easy crossing into excessive and usurious interest. In Y. III 235 the vārddhushyam is reckoned among the smaller sins.

A certain list of low born people is given us from whom the Br. may receive food. A tillage man (ārdhika = ardhasīrin with Yāj.), a cowherd, slave, and a barber, are among the Çūdras those whose food may be eaten, and one who offers himself as a servant IV 253 (so Y. I 166).

The gradual restriction of formerly universal privileges meets us in comparing under this head M. VIII 339 with Y. II 166. In the first case «Manu declares it is no theft» to take roots, fruit, wood etc., thus giving a general rule, in Y. however this privilege is stated as that of the dvija alone.

The Br. has before the formation of the law even offered sacrifices (and so obtained dakshiṇā) from a Çūdra. For in XI 42 the law reads: those who obtain wealth through sacrificing for a Çūdra are blamed by the Brahmavādins as Çūdra-ṛtvijs, in 43 they are termed «ignorant». That this is not a mere possible crime mentioned by Manu to be disparaged is shown by III 178 where loss of all advantage is ordained for him who offers gifts to a çūdrayājaka. In Y.'s list I 222 he is not mentioned but vrātyayājaka occurs III 289 cf. M. XI 198.[1])

With like disparagement are those priests spoken of who sacrifice for a village, grāma, in IV 205 (K. bahūnām

1) And 199 vedam viplāvya probably refers to making known the Veda to those not entitled to hear it.

yâjaka) cf. Y. I 163 and on the other hand in the same çloka mention is made of açrotriya priests which may mean really an unlearned Br. as Kull. takes it or may possibly refer to unbrahmanic priests since çrotriya occurs as designation of Br. in general. In II 206 the law of conduct is laid down for teachers of the same caste vidyāgurushu — nityā vṛttiḥ svayonishu which by implication of those not of the same caste may here be mentioned. If we take the last word as a separate clause as Kull. pitṛvyādishu (of his relatives) whom Jones follows, we are left without a connective particle which is regularly supplied in the next half verse and should not fail here. Yoni is used often enough of caste. I have already (p. 37) noted the occurrence of Çūdra teacher, gaṇānām yājaka, and others. The frequent occurrence of these expressions makes it, I think, evident that these irregularities were not of infrequent occurrence.[1]) That the Br. is mentioned as unfitted for çrāddha if he is Çūdra-yājaka is counterbalanced by a prohibition at the same ceremony of the pupil of a Çūdra and his Guru. In this the text would appear to indicate the possibility of a Çūdra's being a teacher. It is explained by Kull. as «teacher in grammar» etc. thus excluding Veda (III 156). But that teaching the Veda is permitted others than the Br. is evident from the second book II 241—242 «Abrāhmaṇād adhyayanam āpatkāle vidhīyate» restricted thus to time of necessity but then not only permitted but *enjoined.* The student of the low-caste instructor is also required to pay the teacher as long as the instruction continues the same dutiful attendance and obedience as to his Guru — but he should not dwell till his life's end with such a Guru. Kull. declares abrāhmaṇāt to mean one of the twice born not a Brāhm., and further, first a Ksh. and then a Vaiç. is to be preferred, if there is no Br. No such arrangement is in the text. Important to note is the fact that Y. does not seem to have considered the possibility of such an āpatkāla at all.

1) In X 109: Teaching the Veda is preferred to the reception of gifts — in either case we are to understand an otherwise prohibited allowance — āpat case — i. e. improper sacrifices were more lightly regarded than improper reception. 110 must be a gloss.

It would seem, contrary to K.'s opinion, that the Çūdra is distinctly implied, for in the foregoing verses, those immediately before this rule, we are informed that «a believer may receive çubhām vidyām from even a low-born man (avarād api) and the highest virtue from an antya or lowest man, just as one can receive a jewel of a wife from a miserable family. K. translates avarāt with çūdrāt and antyāt with caṇḍālāt — to avoid the logical consequence upon the interpretation of the following çlokas however K. says: mokshopāyam ātmajñānam (ādadīta) for paraṃ dharmam (238). Considering the dharma as spiritual and not Veda — he quotes also Medhātithi who escapes the difficulty by rendering par. dhar. with laukikaṃ vastu! The true meaning is that the Br. may if necessary learn of the Çūdra and the first quotation II 241 is an addition to this. The comparisons with which this injunction is given do not flatter the low-born teacher (cf. 239) [1]).

In general the rule in X 1 stands opposed to this, where only the Br. is acknowledged as teacher; this is however not in respect to āpat cases. So similar to the above, though only in a general sense, we have a statement in II 223; the Br. should imitate anything that is good even if the example be set by one of no honour, yadi strī yadyavarajaḥ (K. çūdrovā) çreyaḥ kiñcit samācaret. It is perhaps a mere accidental juxtaposition which leads us to the logical inference that even in Yāj. Çūdra teachers were current (?) cf. II 135—136. Among the possible heirs of the deceased are mentioned çishya and sabrahmacārin, thus the scholar and school-comrade of deceased, thereupon the addition sarvavarṇeshv ayam vidhiḥ!

The Br. as best among the other castes is represented in X 1. 2. 3. On account of his natural superiority, his distinguished birth, his holding the (niyama) law, and his different saṃskāra (!) the Br. is the superior of the other castes (3). The Br. and no other should explain the Veda, the three other castes abide by their own duties (1). The Br. must understand what the other castes should do, and ex-

1) Çat. 4. 2. 4. 1. one may learn even from a caraka.

plain this to them, and abide himself by these laws (2). According also to I 103 the Br. may explain the scriptures to no one except a twice born man: vidushā Br. idam (law and sacred learning) adhyetavyam . . . . çishyebhaçca pravaktavyam . . . na anyena kenacit, i. e. the Br. explains only to (dvija) pupils, and he alone may explain it.

The Br. is absolute master of his slave's property, VIII 416: The wife, son, and dāsa are three who are adhanāḥ smṛtāḥ, the relation is concisely stated yasya te tasya taddhanam. The property of the Çūd. may be appropriated without hesitation by his master, for he possesses nothing (417). This is in the case of his own slave, but the Çūdra is bodily his master's whether bought or not, or freed. VIII 413—414: A Çūdra bought or not he may cause to do slave's work; for he was created to serve Br. If freed by his master he is not released from his state of slavery. His natural condition, who can take from him?

The penalty for offence against the Br. where the caste is directly stated is generally very severe. More than the law a limb for a limb is the penalty for offences from a Çūdra to a Br. If a low-born man (antyaja K. Çūdra) injure a çreshṭha with any limb he shall have it cut off (chettavyam) VIII 279 and 280 chedanam arhati (cutting off or simply cutting fr. 281) cf. VIII 334. Yāj. II 215. Half the foot should be cut off if one steals the cattle of the Br. kāryo'rdhapādikaḥ VIII 325. In IX 248 we are told that a king should kill an avaravarṇaja with various methods of slaughter that will cause fear (K. among others for instance through chopping off hands and other limbs) on his voluntarily injuring the Br. Amputation or cutting is an ordinary punishment for slight offences and for low personal insults VIII 282, 283 and VIII 270, and 271; a once born insulting a twice born should receive a slit in his tongue, being jaghanyaprabhavaḥ, mocking him with insult in regard to his name an iron rod ten fingers long should be put into his mouth. A low-born man attempting to sit with a higher born (281) (apakṛshṭaja and utkṛshṭa, K. Çūd. and Br.) he shall be branded on the hip with amputation of sphij (as alternative to banishment if he does not die under the branding acc. to K.). Hot oil should be poured into his mouth and ear (ergo death?) if through presumption he insults the Br. by telling him his duty (272).

These practical retributions will have been observed to be mainly from one book. In the eleventh book we have penalties of another kind. XI 205: If one says Hūm to a Br. or Thou to a more reverend person let him, after bathing and fasting the rest of the day, appease the offended one (hūm tūshṇīm sthīyatām iti ākshepam brāhmaṇasya kṛtvā K.). This penance is perhaps intended only for the dvija. Further: (206) If he strike him even with a blade of grass[1]), or fasten him by the neck with a garment, or if he overpower him in debate, let him fall down and appease him, but (207) if he threaten him or strike him with the intention of killing him he goes to hell a hundred or a thousand years (respectively). The striker and drawer of blood remains in hell as many years as the Br. can collect blood-drops on the ground (v. IV 168 w. above p. 27) (cf. Y. III 292). But even the slayer of a Br. is purified by the proper religious exercises (K. says women, Çūdra, etc. are excluded here), IX 249. Yāj. says however that though Veda-study destroy all sin (cf. M. XI 246), yet the slaughter of the Br. is the one sin which is not expunged by a thousand repetitions of the Gāyatrī, gazing at the sun, passing the night in water and living on air by day III 312 (but w. M. in general in 311). XI 68 Brāhmaṇasya rujaḥ kṛtyā — jātibhraṃçakaraṃ smṛtam, but this can be annulled (125) by sāntapana kṛcchra, or if unintentional by Prajāpati penance (cf. 212—213 flg.).

The slaughter of a Br. is naturally mentioned among the mahānti pātakāni[2]) (XI 55. IX 235. Y. III 227) and the associates of such evil doers are reckoned equal to the sinners themselves. Under these the Br. are included with the rest of the castes. But for slaugther of a Br. we have a list of expiations in XI 73 flg. Twelve years let the Br. slayer dwell in a hut in the forest eating alms to purify

1) Cf. IV 166. 169 v. above p. 19.

2) That of Çūd. Vaiç. and Ksh. however as upapātakam XI 67.

his soul with, a skull as a sign[1]), or (if Ksh. K.) he may die by exposing himself to archers or to fire, or (if a king K.) he may give sacrifices, or (if a priest) make a pilgrimage or give up all his possessions to a wise Br., or by rescuing the life of a Br. or cow etc.[2]), or finally by stating his crime at a hayamedha to Br. and Ksh. (v. p. 45) for (84) Dharmasya Br. mūlam agram rājanya ucyate — since the Br. is the root and the Ksh. the top of the law he is purified by declaring the sin there. These expiations are for unintentional murder, but XI 90: kāmato Brāhmaṇavadhe nishkṛtir na vidhīyate. There is no expiation (K. explains by making iyam of foregoing verse stand with nishkṛtiḥ, this expiation is not enough for intentional slaughter; it must be doubled etc.) cf. Y. III 243 flg. The same expiations are enjoined for unjust accusation of Guru (89).

Between the Br. and an outcast there should not be the slightest connection even if in necessity, neither a religious nor a family connection II 40. In the house of a Br. no one of the lower castes is considered a guest. Na Brāhmaṇasya tu atithir gṛhe rājanya ucyate vaiçyaçūdrau — likewise a friend, kinsman, Guru, do not pass as guests, III 110 (K. The first because of lower birth, by same rule only a Br. and Ksh. are guests of a Ksh. and only Br. Ksh. Vaiç. of a Vaiç.). But he must receive the Vaiç. and Çūd. if they come to his house as guests and he shall let them eat with the servants (after the Br. and Ksh.). The Vaiç. and Çūd. are here placed on a level with each other, they are both to eat with servants, III 112. In presence of Çūd. one must not read the Veda IV 99. Y. (I 148) adds also one of lowest castes and one expelled from castes. The Br. must not give advice to Çūdra, nor ucchishṭam, nor havis, nor instruct him in right, nor show him the law (except his dāsa K.) IV 80 cf. X 125. Three days must the Br. drink kuça water if he has drunk water left by a

1) K. says this general statement is to be restricted to the Br. If Ksh. Vaiç. and Çūd. do the same deed their punishment is respectively twice, thrice, or four times as long. The sin is here akāmataḥ.

2) The purification of those dying for a cow or Br. is declared in V 95 to be instantaneous.

Çūd. XI 149. Eating what is left by a woman or Çūd. he must drink barley-water for seven nights XI 153. The Br. is not to go alone with a Vṛshala nor mock one jātihīna IV 140—141. The last clause seems to show more compassion than contempt for the men of low caste. The broken pieces at a çrāddha given to a Vṛshala causes the giver to go to hell. III 249.

The Çūdra must not carry out a dead Br. V 104 (so long as his own caste is present). This would prevent the Br.'s going to heaven: asvargyā hyāhutiḥ — çūdrasaṃsparçadūshitā.

The Br. must do penance for involuntary slaughter of (Ksh. v. below) the lower castes in ratio to the time for killing a Br. i. e. for a good Vaiç. one year's penance and a fine, and for Çūd. six months' penance or a fine[1]) XI 130. 131. cf. Y. III 266—7.

Even for maligning a (Ksh.) Vaiç. or a Çūdra the priest is to be fined. Half of that for defaming the Ksh. is to be given for a similar offence against the Vaiçya (thus 25 paṇas) and in the case of a Çūdra the fine is then twelve VIII 268. Little as is the fine it is still important, for the very fact of enjoining a fine upon insulting one whom the Br., as popularly represented, needs to treat with no respect or consideration has a significance. It follows from this that as far as the letter of the law goes the Çūdra has precise rights in his relations with even the highest caste. In Yāj. II 206 we find as shown on p. 14 only a general regulation that the infliction of punishment is to follow varṇajātyuttarādharaiḥ, and in Gaut. XII 13 this liability in case of the Çūd. is expressly withdrawn.

Any one of those not belonging to the Br. caste is to be killed (prāṇāntam daṇḍam arhati) if he is guilty of inchastity VIII 359. This rule in view of its extreme rigour may be regarded as belonging to one of the oldest portions of the law.

The simple text does not authorize the insertion of the

1) In Vaiç. the connective in M. is ca, in Çūd. vā, only a fine is mentioned in Āpast. 1. 9. 24. (1, 2, 3).

passage in this paragraph at all; for it is evidently an old law of general application, where only the Br. is excluded, and he in this case, with the definition from 379 quoted above (mauṇḍyam prāṇāntiko daṇḍo Br.sya), does not escape without disgrace. But this çloka may serve as a fine example of the inaccurate statements we obtain by trusting to the commentator, for Kull. in his endeavour to reconcile this universal law with the later more carefully graded punishment for such a crime first interprets abrāhmaṇaḥ as Çūdra, for which we have no ground at all, and is for instance otherwise translated by K. himself, ex. gr. II 241—242 as Ksh. and Vaiç. (where there is as little reason for excluding the Çūd. as here for excluding the Ksh. Vaiç.), and in VII 85 the word cannot mean a Çūdra. Moreover K. adds that the crime is with an unwilling Br. woman which is a pure hypothesis grounded on other çlokas. It is unnecessary to add that Sir William Jones accepts in his translation these unauthorized additions of his Magnus Apollo. 1)

The Çūdra, adhyadhīna, (K. dāsa, rightly) has the right of representing his master in business transactions VIII 167; even the adhyadhīna may transact business for the benefit of the family when his master is at home or abroad and the master must not rescind the transaction. This is however denied in general terms by 199 same book, sale . . . made by one not the (real) owner is declared invalid. This second rule is upheld by Yāj. II 168 — The first case not being mentioned by him is therefore included under passage parallel to second.

The perhaps most remarkable passage in which the action of the Br. is influenced by the low castes is the doubtful morality propounded in VIII 104. Here the teaching is formulated that falsehood, respect. perjury, is to be practiced in trials at court wherever speaking the truth would cause the death of a Vipra, Ksh. Vaiç. or *Çūdra*.

1) Loiseleur Deslongchamps also: Un soûdra — — pour avoir fait violence à la femme d'un Brâhmane — and in both translations there is nothing to show that the two restrictive clauses are not a part of the original!

In this case perjury is even better than the truth (cf. Y. II 83). K. refers to VIII 380 and quotes Gautama (XIII 24. 25). Na tu pāpīyaso jīvanam (tadadhīnam) to show that extreme criminals are not permitted the benefit of this law. The very wise Br. are indeed not included here, since they are excluded as witnesses, but the ordinary Br. and the other castes (except king in Ksh.) are here enjoined to perjure themselves even for a Çūdra. (The sentiment may be compared with Soph. Phil. 108. 109!) The young student is no better than a Çūdra until he is born of the Veda II 172 (svadhāni-nayanādṛte) except in certain cases, until then he is çūdreṇa samaḥ — relative to uttering the holy texts.

The Br. is in IV 224—225 compared with a money lender, a case that may be added to those quoted above to show that the Br.'s character is more important than his caste in securing him veneration. The gods regarding both the food of a learned Br. who is stingy, and of an usurer who is generous, declared «it is the same», but Prajāpati coming (to them) said: make not the unequal equal, the liberal man's food is purified by faith, but that of the other (the Br.) is destroyed through unfaith. Cf. Y. I 203 yācitena dātavyam *çraddhāpūtam*.

IV. The Kshatriya:

a) The general regulations for the Ksh. have already been given under the head of the four castes, the twice born castes, and on occasion under the other divisions. We can naturally not look for any such fullness in general details as in the Br. caste. The chief interest of the caste centers about the king and the regulations for the Ksh. are when universal better grouped under the head of mutual relations. In regard to the general occupations of the Ksh. we have only to add the specific injunction in X 77 that the three duties of the Br. teaching, sacrificing for others, and receiving gifts, cease with the Ksh., and that in regard to a change of castes the Ksh. may, as before noted, assume the occupation of Vaiç. (or Çūdra) but X 95 is strictly forbidden to live as a Br. (Na tu . . jyāyasīm vṛttim abhimanyeta karhicit). What the strength of this law was in time of distress we have discussed above. The Ksh. is made pure, his highest sacrifice is performed, if he is struck down in battle, while performing his military duty, with outstretched weapons V 98.

From not reciprocal connection with Br. we add to the clauses above that the Ksh. like the other castes is not regarded as a guest in the house of the Br., but the latter treats him entirely differently from the treatment he gives the Vaiç. For general laws however of the Ksh. we pass rather to the mutual relations, where the rules for Ksh. as universally laid down, and his treatment of his fellow Ksh., are scarcely to be separated. (b). *Ksh. and Ksh.* Scanty as is the information in regard to the common Ksh. the regulations are nevertheless of great interest. We learn first in regard to the Ksh. as warrior, that those are to be preferred who have come from (kurukshetra, matsyās etc.) the same districts which are in II 19 noted as being the homes of the most respected Brahmans. We are also told that the king should select tall and light men, the characteristic probably of the soldiers of those districts.[1]) These warriors he should place in the van VII 193.

The rules of warfare for the Ksh. are in the highest degree noble and humane. VII 90 flg. Let him engaged in battle (yudhyamāna) not kill his enemies in fight with pointed weapons (or deceitful, P. W. kūṭair āyudhaiḥ) nor with ear-shaped darts (karṇibhiḥ — K. karṇyākāraphalakair bāṇaiḥ. This seems to mean a dart or lance so shaped that being flat and pointed the barb intensifies the wound on withdrawing the haft), nor with anointed (poisoned) weapons, nor with weapons glowing with fire. Nor (when he is himself in his chariot, Kull.) let him kill one who has dismounted, nor should he kill a eunuch, nor one who cries for mercy (takes a suppliant attitude kṛtāñjali) nor one whose hair has become unloosened, nor one who has seated himself, nor one who says «I am thine», nor one who is asleep, nor one who is without defence or weapon, or is naked, or a non-fighter who is looking on, nor one who is fighting

1) Kull. takes these as *not* inhabitants of the counties mentioned, but of others.

with another, nor one who has met a misfortune with his arms, nor one off his guard, nor one who is ill or afraid, nor one who is wounded (atiparikshatam — bahuprahārākulam K.).

These rules of conduct seem also to have been strictly observed in practice — compare the scene in Mbhā. (14. 81. 9 = 2410) where Ulūpī blames Arjuna for killing Bhīshma against the law of warriors; for by such law every trick is forbidden, and he who had lowered his weapons should not be killed, and every mixture of a third in a fight between two is forbidden.[1]) Also we find the astradharma quoted (7. 142. 71 = 5949) as forbidding the attacking of one not on his guard, so Karṇa cries to Arjuna when busied with his chariot (8. 90. 105 = 4734). No brave hero shoots at him who has laid aside his arms.[2])

The soldier who obtains possession of chariot, or horse, or elephant, or private personal property, or cattle, or women, or the base metals, possesses them as his own: yo yaj jayati tasya tat is the brief rule appended to the list VII 96; but they should give the king the choice of the good since this is vaidic law (97) (cf. Kull.). The king should give to all the soldiers that which has been captured by no one in particular (apṛthagjitam). According to K. the uddhāra of the king is in respect to the best goods taken — gold, silver, land, and, in contradiction to 96, the elephants, horses, and cattle, even the chariots — to support which K. quotes Gautama X 21 vāhanañca rājñaḥ. Çloka 96 seems to be the original simple law of warfare, what each got he could keep, the king's share not being regarded, while 97 limits this general usage. The captured women neither in Gaut. nor K. to Manu fall as spoil to the king.

Something from the common soldiers may perhaps be drawn from VII 69—70 flg. we are told that a fort (durga) is considered as the best defence since a bowman placed on a rampart (prākāra) can give fight to an hundred men. These seem to be therefore the favourite soldiers, coupled with the remark quoted as to the warriors who are tall and light

1) V. Adolph Holtzmann Arjuna S. 30.
2) Ib. S. 37 & 49.

we may draw the conclusion that the battle was more in the form of light skirmishing than in massing the men in heavy squadrons.

To this we may add the position which the king as chief of the Ksh. takes in relation to his army, and the notes we can gather of the army itself in this respect. In examining the part which the king plays in regard to his troops and army in general, we are struck with the extreme simplicity which characterizes the whole intercourse between the head of state and the soldiers.

The king has the personal supervision of all that concerns his forces, as well as that of income etc. *Every day* the king must make an inspection of business — and of his chariots, of his income and expenses, mines and treasury, VIII 419. He reviews the army in person and examines all the chariots, arms, and ornaments VII 222. Y. I 328.

In certain cases the king divides his command with the officers; for in VII 173 we are told he is to divide his force (dvidhā balaṃ kṛtvā) and in VII 167 we learn he is to make a separation of the army for the sake of gaining some particular point (balasya svāminaçca eva sthitiḥ kāryārthasiddhaye) and here we may add the different forms of order in which the battle array is to be drawn up when on the march. He is to advance, namely, daṇḍavyūhena (VII 187) (and here as in the other cases acc. to K. the king is to remain in the most sheltered spot when danger is feared (bhaye sati)) farther, either in the form of a waggon, or of a boar, or dolphin, or like a needle, or Garuḍa (K. pṛthutaramadhyaḥ).[1] The king and chief general alter their respective positions acc. to K. as the form of the army and safety require. In the next çloka VII 188 we are told that the king is to place himself padmena . . vyūhena, extending his army wherever he fears danger.

The art of peace and war making, the kinds of marching and encamping, are briefly described in VII 160 flg.

1) Çl. 191 seems an addition to this. Let him fight arraying his men in the form of a needle or a thunderbolt. In the same çloka he is directed to form little squadrons or if he has many men to disperse them vistārayet i. e. not in compact order.

These give no light however on the comparative station of king and army. In general the king is to avoid casting his fortunes on a battle (yuddhaṃ vivarjayet) since the result if disastrous is apt to be a too decisive overthrow. The time for going to war is mentioned in 182 coupled with the injunction in 183 that any time is to be seized if he is sure of victory. Not only has the king the personal supervision of the troops in time of peace but he must aid in encouragement of his troops while in action. He is to exhort and inspire his army when in battle array (praharshayed balaṃ vyūhya) examining them personally as well as taking notice of their conduct during the fighting VII 194. It appears however that the king though on the ground during the battle is not to front the battle; we may draw this conclusion from the «lotus» array quoted above in which he is to ensconce himself. The adhipati or chief general seems therefore to be the practical leader of the acting troops, except in the case where the rule is divided as mentioned above. VII 189 The king sends the senāpati and leaders in every direction during the fighting. The king must also place small divisions or squads (gulmāḥ) here and there during the fighting, men who are well fitted, quick-witted, capable of standing or fighting, and fearless, and who do not play false. (190) The only arms which the soldiers use are bows, swords, and shields, carma, with weapons (āyudhāḥ) in general, added to these, but no others specifically mentioned. Waggons, horses, boats, and elephants are recommended respectively for level land and morass. The bows, cāpa, are for wooded ground, the others for open ground, VII 192[1]). In 74 we have seen the bowman preferred for a fort — here dhanur(dhara). The gulma mentioned above is used in a different sense in VII 114—123. Here we have an arrangement corresponding to armed garrisons which are to be placed over the whole land in time of peace, and seem in fact to be a royal police; for the description represents these

1) In VII 185 the sixfold army (shaḍvidham balam) may be explanatory of the parts or of the form in 187. There are three means of reducing an enemy, sāmnā, dānena, bhedena VII 198.

gulma as being stationed over different numbers of villages, and indeed in an ascending scale. Namely, over two, three, or five, and so over an hundred, corresponding to these there should be an adhipati appointed over each village, and over groups of ten, twenty, an hundred, or a thousand villages. The gulma are termed rāshṭrasya saṃgraha, that is they are intended for the purpose of restraining violence, and preserving order in the state. The arrangements in regard to the adhipati and gulma do not precisely agree, but the number of the gulma is loosely stated. The command ascends from the smaller circles to the generals over the large divisions forming a graded power from the grāmasyādhipati to the king himself. The lower must notify his superior of all the evils (dosha) arising under his government. Their pay is drawn from the villages over which they rule and the amount is proportioned to the extent of command (118 flg.) In each city the king appoints beside these a sarvārthacintaka whose duty is to have a general oversight of affairs. Spies are to be employed to render the security of the state complete by keeping a watch on the officers thus appointed because, a candid admission, these ministers placed in power are generally rascals (çaṭha), and he should protect his people from them. So Y. I 337 The gulmas are mentioned in the same way in IX 266 where the taskaras, robbers, are to be detected.[1]) This system of graded rule among officers appointed by the king in time of peace is the only insight we have in Manu into the relations of the king's lords. Of relations between the officers in the army, or what position they held in regard to the common soldier we can determine nothing.

We pass rather to the position of the king and can include at one and the same time the general statements in respect to the king himself, and those which bring him in connection with his subjects — statements which are hard to separate, as the king in India more than any where else is, according to the law, a being created for the good of his people,

1) Acc. to Āpast. II 10. 26. 4: The men in this capacity are from either Vaiç. Ksh. or Br. caste.

and is not regarded in the least as a despot, whose existence is sufficient unto himself, but much more as a father of his people.

The king is divine. This statement is given more than once. VII 8. Even when a child a king is not to be despised; for he is a great divinity in the form of a man (mahatī Devatā hi eshā nararūpeṇa). The composition of this divinity is expounded in V 96. The body of the king consists of parts of Soma Agni Arka Anila Indra Vittapatī (K. Kubera [v. VII 42] and Varuṇa) and Yama the eight guardians of the world. In VII 3. 4. the same list is given (Vitteça = Vittapati, Candra = Soma) with the addition of Varuṇa, who now appears expressly mentioned. In the first case the king's form, vapus, consists of these divinities, in the second the creator produces him by collecting particles of the same, the second seems to refer to the spirit as well as body, the latter only, to the first. In VII 7 he is accordingly identified with the gods one after the other, «he is Agni and Vāyu, he (is) the sun and moon, he (is) Yama (dharmarāj), he (is) Kubera, he Varuṇa, he great Indra» and upon this identification of the king with the gods in general follows the verse quoted first where he is resolved into the godhead itself — one must not imagine he is only a man, Na avamantavyo «manushya» iti.

He is also representative of the four ages — when the king sleeps he is the kali yugam, awake he is the dvāparaṃ yugam — engaged in business he is the tretā yugam, going to war he is kṛtaṃ yugam IX 301—302 (vicaran defined by K. yadā . . . yathā çāstram punaḥ karmāṇi anutishṭhan vicarati tadā kṛty°. Jones «living virtuously». B. R. In's feld ziehen, einen angriff machen, and comp. Ait. Br. 7. 14.[1])

The king is directed to imitate the various functions of the above mentioned divinities — to whom Pṛthivī is added. As Indra rains for four mouths, so let the king rain pleasures over his realm; as Āditya (arka) draws up the water for eight months with his rays, so let him draw the taxes from his people; as the Maruts (vāyu) enter all beings in

1) Cf. Ind. Stud. I 286 & 460.

moving, so (by means of his spies) he should be everywhere; and as Yama directs friend and enemies at the proper time, so the subjects should be governed by the king; as one is fastened by Varuṇa in chains, so let him restrain the wicked; as men seeing the full moon are glad, so that king is like Candra, whose subjects are glad. Endowed with heat (majesty) and glow (glory) against evil doers, and killing his wicked vassals he is like Agni,[1]) and as Dharā (dhārayate) upholds all creatures, so upholding all creatures he is like Pṛthivī IX 303—311. The tertium comparationis is occasionally a little overloaded — The taxes are not restrained to eight months, nor should we suppose that the king is to rain upon his realm with pleasures for only four. The passage however bears marks of being a later addition.

The king is also pure: Na rājñām aghadosh o'sti V 93; so V 97 Na asya (rājñaḥ) açaucam vidhīyate. So Y. III 27 mahīpatīnām na açaucam.

The highest duty of kings, and that which gives them the greatest felicity, is in battle never to retreat, to protect the people, and to be obedient to the Br. VII 88. This is a most remarkable passage; for the servile obedience here demanded of the king toward the Br. is expressed in the same phrase which generally characterizes the position of the Çūdra toward the upper castes — çuçrūshā. Y. I 322 gives this again with the words «giving that which has been secured in war to the Br.»[2]) — this is the highest duty of kings. K. explains by paricaryā. From the foregoing çlokas in Manu we should be tempted to transpose the words of K. as an equivalent of the çuçrūshā in this çloka. The expression is at least otherwise unparalleled in our author, unless we compare çāsane VII 37 v. below.[3])

That one of the chief functions of the king is to support

1) The king warms eyes and minds like the sun. No one can gaze upon him VII 6.

2) M. IX 323 the king gives the money arising from fines to the Br. (sarvadaṇḍasamutthita).

3) Sanpūjayet in VII 201 is more of general honouring; çuçrūshitvā is used of the Br.'s conduct toward the cows in XI 111 but with namaskṛtya.

and protect his people, has been alluded to in the similies quoted above, more specifically we have VII 35. The king is created as the protector of all the castes in order, and all the stadia of the Br. life. Cf. VII 3. The king is here said to be created rakshārtham asya sarvasya. As guardian VII 17 he is purushodaṇḍaḥ — sa netā çāsitā ca saḥ.

The king is not only to have regard for his own people but he must also show consideration for those whom he conquers. VII 201: on conquering another country let the king honour the gods (of that country K.) and the just Br.; let him also give pardon (general immunity) and make proclamations of gentle import (khyāpayed abhayāni).[1] After placing one of his own race over the conquered people (202), let him make ordinances and laws for them as prescribed (203) (in their lawbooks, K.). Cf. Y. I 342 In spite of the agreement with the ordinance of Y. it seems to me that the explanation of K. (in 203) is not correct. The use of kurvīta appears to point to the establishment of new laws (new to the conquered) and not to the retention of the old observances. The genitive teshām does not necessarily apply to the laws or customs called yathā uditāḥ and much more this expression is when unaccompanied by restrictions the general term for referring to the laws of Manu. The word paripālyo 'sau(ācāraḥ) used by Yāj. in the parallel passages gives the meaning here sought by K. for M., but exactly the difference between kar and pālay makes a ground for our belief that the new country is in M. to be brought under subjection to the laws given in the Mān. dh. çās., not that he should «make» laws (which were already made) in accordance with the precepts of the conquered race.

At the end of his life the king is to seek death in battle — after giving his wealth (v. last page) to the Br. and bestowing his kingdom on his son. IX 323, or die acc. to K. anaçanādinā, by starvation or a similar death.

The king must personally be competent to judge of the various matters in his realm. He must be acquainted with the trayī vidyā, with the system of punishment and politics,

1) Abhayāni is γῆς ἄδεια.

he must also be a logician and a philosopher, and he must learn from the people (lokataḥ) the matters concerning trade and business VII 43. Opposed to this which he should know are in 45 flg. a list of vices he should shun, ten arising from lust and seven from temper. In 50 we are informed that drinking, gambling (dice), women, and hunting, are the chief of the first — and of the second, relaxation of punishment, and injury through word or ill use of power (pārushya rough treatment) — of these seven each is worse than the next (51. 52). The third and fourth however (striyaḥ — mṛgayā) seem to have been as a matter of fact much more lightly regarded. Corresponding to the knowledge which the king is bound to be acquainted with, we have in VII 154 the utterance: The king should consider kṛtsnañ ca ashṭavidhaṃ karma pañcavargañca tattvataḥ together with the friendliness, the dislike, and the conduct of the land which lies about him. It seems from the calculations which follow that there are in all seventy-two objects to which the king must attend; these are obtained by applying the five objects of concern: minister, realm, city (or fort), wealth, army to twelve persons — the middle, that is those occupying the ground between him and his enemy [1]), the one who is bent on conquering, the neutrals, and his foe (these elements form the mūlam maṇḍalasya); and the eight others numbered with these (= 12). Apply the five concerns (v. above) to each and one has altogether seventy-two; that is, acc. to K., one must add the four mūlaprakṛtayaḥ of 155, and the eight in 156, to the sixty obtained by the process explained. What this eight means in 156 is not so clear, acc. to K. the friend, foe's friend, friend's friend, friend of the friend of his foe and also (four) the pārshṇigrāha, ākranda, pārshṇigrāhāsāra, and ākrandāsāra. The second group however is only found in part in çl. 207, and previously there is no list like the first — ākranda is further (in 207) declared by P.W. to have no personal meaning. If we take the «eight others» as applicable to the divisions of the eight-fold action we must reject Kull.'s explanation of the same since the five of 157 cannot be combined with them.

1) If we translate *madhyama* with P.W. as neutral what antithesis lies between the meaning of this word and that of *udāsīna*?

K. explains the eight-fold action as follows 1) reception of taxes 2) The expenses to ministers etc. 3) right or 4) wrong deeds of ministers, 5) oversight of the judicial apartment in case doubt occurs in regard to debts etc., 6) punishment of wrong doers who have offended in a point of law, 7) purification from wickedness, 8) when this has taken place, the prāyaçcittam for the crime. Pañcavarga is also acc. to K. pañcavidha *cāra* varga, explained 1) kāpaṭika — deceivers, 2) pravrajyārūḍhapatita (udāsthita) — fallen priests who have abandoned their vows, 3) karshakaḥ kshīṇavṛttiḥ decayed farmers, 4) vāṇijaka kshī° likewise such merchants, 5) muṇḍojaṭilo vā vṛttikāmas tāpasavyañjanaḥ even priests under guise of religion.[1]) Interesting as this list is it can not be accepted as explaining this çloka — for it implies that all these occupations and the spies were so well known that they had become unnecessary to note, and that the «eight-fold action» would with the «division of five» be self explanatory. I think it is evident that there is more here than belonged here originally and the interpolation is easily explained. For the first half of çloka 155 is rendered suspicious by the fact that the words pracārañca . . . ca ceshṭitam occur in the second çloka before in exactly the same position and moreover the separation of vijigīshu from the çatru is a weak one, the first embracing the second and the second implying the first. If now we consider that the first half of çloka 154 is not self explanatory, and is not explainable from the text, at least as far as pañcavarga goes, and that the same numbers appear as said a few çl. later in another connection I think it seems evident that this does not have a right to stand as a part of the original. If we unite the two half çlokas left 154 b and 155 b we have a connected series which suits the text. We then have the disposition and conduct of the land, (dual as one) the conduct of the neutrals, and that of his foes — these form the mūlam maṇḍalasya and with the other eight make twelve. The lack of division before the num-

1) The spies play a not inconsiderable part in the royal nīti of Manu, but we find no such division. They are used as well for detectives as for army spies. In IX 256 the king is called cāracakshur mahīpatiḥ. Cf. VII 184; IX 261; also IX 298; and IX 306 and IX 266.

bering here is no more abrupt than as the text now stands and there is further to notice that *as* the text now stands we must not reckon 154 b in with 155 or the number four necessary to make the twelve arrived at is exceeded, but how can we banish the «conduct of the surrounding land» (154 b) from those elements which consitute the mūlam of it? The repetition of pracāra is lessened by one in this arrangement, as the text now stands we have it repeated four times in three çlokas. After these we have the addition in regard to the five (minister etc.) and then the false reckoning that $5 \times 12 = 72$ which is alone to be obtained from the text, and K.'s supposition that we are to add each factor for itself is merely an ingenious escape, besides after the king has for instance examined (applying the five to çatru) the minister, realm, fortress, treasury, army, there is little more to seek in the individual himself but, whether or not, the statement is, however we interpret it, *not in the text*, and seventy-two is therefore false. Moreover in accepting this we must take K.'s explanation of ashṭau — but this is very far fetched, and moreover raises distrust when we consider that two «eights» are here in play, the eight duties in 154 which he explains in other ways, and finally these eight which are mentioned as if well known (ashṭaucānyāḥ), but which he must explain by taking allusions fifty çlokas ahead. It seems almost impossible under these circumstances to allow 157 b to stand, since the minister etc. do not suit the context, but this must be regarded as not genuine — the false arithmetic, the impossibility of explanation except by the plainly desperate attempt of the Commentator, is enough to warrant rejection — we must either regard the first half of the verse as together with the second half interpolated, or it stands alone independent of the foregoing, and represents another set of objects for the king's attention — The verse reminds us of IX 294.

The authority of the king in effecting new laws is limited by the local and family regulations as well as by the institutions of the various castes. This point which is of weight if we reflect upon the wide province which these restrictions cover, and the decided check given thereby to autocratic supremacy, is stated as follows in VII 146 sadbhir ācaritaṃ yat syād dhārmikaiçca dvijātibhiḥ tad deçakulajātīnām aviruddhan prakalpayet. The logical converse is therefore that every practice which (is in itself bad or) interferes with the laws of the locality, family or caste the king has no right to alter. Deça does not refer to other lands which might be cited as an argument for K.'s interpretation of VII 203 (v. above p. 68) for the restrictions here are not in case of war but in the king's own country, compare VIII 41 jātijānapadān dharmān çreṇīdharmāṃçca samīkshya kuladharmāṃçca svadharman pratipādayet — Y. I 360 and II 192: The king shall protect their former manner of life (occupations). Gautama XI 20: These deçajātikuladharmāḥ are declared to be pramāṇam influential as authority. These quotations from the other lawgivers are not however so wide as that from M.; for the former grant that the family caste and local customs are to be regarded in making laws, whereas M. requires that the king's laws are not to collide with these.[1])

In the matter of trade, mentioned among the subjects in which the king is to be conversant, we find the sovereign playing an active part. He must practically be daily busied with these concerns which touch the Vaiçya caste. The king for instance must arrange the worth (price) every five days, or every fortnight, of all the goods which are in market VIII 402 (cf. 401), though from 389 he seems to leave such matters to experts, taking himself a twentieth part arghaprakshepaṇāt (Y. II 261. cf. 251).

The judicial power of the king is generally exclusively confined to consultations with his ministers, but one rather remarkable law presents him in the light of exercising at the same time the judiciary and the executive office.

Two facts from a Manu-standpoint alone point to the truth that this case preserves one of the antique laws, and may be undoubtedly considered as taken from the laws already existing prior to the first recension of the Mān. dh. çās. These are, first, that the formula is repeated twice in different books without essential change of meaning, and, second, that

1) Kula, çreṇi, and Pūga do not appear in M. to have the technical sense later ascribed to these terms.

the king does not have in any other case the power of an executive officer; much more, a certain set of men are according to laws, which from their position we may assume to be later, set aside for the especial office which the king here fills, and that this office is one only belonging to a low mixed caste. The king has indeed in this description the position of a petty chief of a lawless tribe far different from that which we elsewhere see in the well ordered courts of justice as it meets us elsewhere in the eighth book.

The case is in regard to the punishment of a thief. It is first stated in VIII 314—316 as follows: The king is to be approached by a thief who runs to him with loosened hair, saying «punish me» (çādhi mām), bringing a club, or a cudgel made of acacia catechu wood, or a spear pointed each end, or an iron rod, on his shoulder. In consequence of punishment or release he is absolved from his theft; but if the king does not strike him he takes himself the burden of the guilt. This, it is to be noticed, is a strictly general law without restriction in regard to the caste of the offender. The second case is found in XI 101. The king seizing a club shall strike (or kill) the thief and by the blow (or by his death) he is purified. But a Br. by penance. In 100 we learn that the offender is a vipra who has stolen gold — Suvarṇasteyakṛdvipro rājānam abhigamya tu. This passage has been however most remarkably handled. In the text we have the Br. represented as the thief in 100, in 101 however an exception of tapas as a penalty is presented the Br. From the Comm. we have the statement that this is the gold of a priest which is stolen, of which there is in the text no evidence[1]) and on the strength of *eva* in 101 he declares the Br. is not to be so punished at all but only to be purified by tapas! and quotes VIII 380. That this passage contradicts the evident interpretation of the text is true but that one passage of Manu can be cited as overthrowing even by a direct negation an implied meaning in another is from the nature of the work impossible.[2]) K.'s

1) Nor so construed by K. in the similar steno vipraḥ of XII 57.

2) Cf. the directly contradictory injunctions in book IX in regard to the conduct of the widow.

explanation is evidently founded on the wish to free the Br. from such a possible disgrace; but were we to reject this explanation altogether, bringing Brāhmaṇaḥ in apposition to stenaḥ in 101 and not in opposition as K. does, we would have a much more rational solution and one better in harmony with the text, i. e. it would then read: the thief who is a Br. is purified by the punishment (blow; death) as he also is by tapas thus giving an alternative. Otherwise what distinction can we make between Br. and the vipraḥ of 100? No other is mentioned in the text. Description of tapas follows in 102. If the priest (dvija) desires to remove the guilt of stealing gold by penance, let him live in a wood performing the penance suitable for the expiation of a slayer of a Br. Here the dvija being used with the desiderative ptc. (apanunutsu) speaks also for the fact of the preceding çl. giving *two expiations for the Br.* Yāj. III 257 inverts the whole situation; for he says «He who takes the gold of a Br.» (It is from this that K.'s note is explainable) whereas M.'s statement can only refer to a Br. who steals gold, whether from another Br. is not said, though it were not impossible to infer it through analogy with the punishment *cared Brahmahaṅovratam* in 102. The three passages appear to represent three distinct stages in the growth of state and society. In the first M. VIII the offender is not a Br. the theft is not one of gold. In the second M. XI the thief is a priest who steals gold — in Y. the theft is from a Br. The different forms of address in M. seem to show alone that the form of the eighth book is the more primitive of the two. Çādhi mām in VIII to the king(!) and in XI mām bhavān anuçāstu. Y. does not give the formula at all.[1])

1) If we compare (these regulations with Āpast. 1. 9. 25. 4. Gaut. 12. 44 we see that the formula is as we draw from M. itself a petrified expression of the older time. Āp. stenaḥ prakīrṇakeço 'ṃse musalam ādāya rājānam gantvā karma cakshīta tena enam hanyāt | vadhe mokshaḥ and as a general law this confirms the lateness of the restrictions of M. and Y. in regard to gold and of a Br. In the same way Gaut. stenaḥ prakīrṇakeçaḥ etc. and pūto vadhamokshābhyām. In G. and Ā. the meaning of vadha corresponding to the verbal equivalent han (v. G. 45)

Incidental mention of the king standing without particular relation to the other castes can only be sparingly

is evidently death — in Ā. seen from the harmony with ib. 6 & 7. We have also the choice here: (6) or he should enter fire — (7) or end his life by deprivation of food. Here we have plainly a case parallel to that where the sinner is freed from sin by dying for a cow or Br. etc. i. e. he receives absolution from the sin but pays for it with his life XI 80. In case he is not punished all authorities agree that the king receives the blame. We must through these preserve the same meaning for the manavic text where vadha and han are also synonymous. Nor does the çās of 315 VIII prevent this, since it is a general term meaning as well punish in the extreme sense as simple corporal punishment. The logical conclusion would be that the king should always kill a thief, which is again in perfect harmony with the manavic law which punishes theft with capital punishment. So we see in Āp. that the options allowed result in death and these must be regarded as on a level with the first. It is not therefore wonderful that K. wishes to ward the death penalty from the Br. by confining his punishment wholly to penance. The legal penalties are however to be held apart from religious penances. As far as we can glean from Gaut. the Br. is here prohibited from the death penalty by the words Na çārīro Brāhmaṇadaṇḍah the simple castigation or other bodily punishment not being here meant as we see from Nāṇkakaraṇa (46. 47) used in opposition to the foregoing. The *alternative* of punishment by the king, or penance, is clearly expressed in Y. ib. 258 *anivedya*. In Āp. one of these alternatives suggests that we may perhaps see in agnim vā praviçet not so much a death penalty, as a form of probatio divina, which fell afterwards wholly to the probatio through the king. It is not indeed a trial of the (already acknowledged) guilt but a test of the severity of punishment due the offender. This would connect with the well known trial of the thief by hot iron in the Chand. Upan. VI 16. 1 & 2 where the thief's guilt is tested. Even vadhe mokshaḥ might imply a reliance upon divine guidance; for the life of the criminal hangs on the chance of the blow, so that the king might be considered a passive agent in the hand of the divinity, his active part consisting only in pardoning, which is, however, through the accompanying retribution practically denied him, so that his whole action represents him as exercising no right of private judgement. But I have already shown that vadha must be interpreted death here so that the fire test would be necessarily grouped in the same category.[1] In regard to the treatment of thieves in general in Manu we find in IX 270 that the king takes no active part in the infliction of punishment, and that the thief is to be killed if he is (captured) with the hoḍha (v. P. W. s. v.); if not, not. Ghātayet is here

1) In regard to trial by fire cf. the punishment in XI 74, as expiation prāsyet ātmānam agnau.

quoted. Some are plagued with others' business — a witness, a bailer, and family, and four accumulate substance, a vipra, a wealthy man, a merchant, and a king (āṭhya K. uttamarṇa) VIII 169. Where an ordinary man (prākṛto janaḥ) would be fined a kārshāpaṇa the king is to be fined a thousand, (K. adds he is to throw it into the water or give it to the Br. cf. IX 243 flg.) VIII 336. cf. Y. II 307 The king is fined thirty times the amount of a fine which he has unjustly taken. The king is by this law not only open to punishment, but his crime is intensified by his station. In VIII 38, 39, in consideration of his affording protection the king receives half of treasures found, and old stores. The king cannot serve as witness on a trial VIII 65. The king even if distressed may not accept what is not to be taken nor though in a flourishing condition should he reject, however small it is, what he ought to receive VIII 170.

IV. c. The relations of the Ksh. and the lower castes find their most important moment, aside from the general protection of the realms by the Ksh., in the regulations of the Ksh., respect. the king, with regard to the power which the royal house possesses in the taxation of his land. A marked tendency is apparent to make the taxes as considerate as circumstances can admit, protection of the people is the ground thought of the law in the limitation of the taxing power. Let the king so ordain the taxes that he and the workman may mutually obtain an advantage yathā phalena yujyeta rājā kartāca karmaṇām VII 128 and in the preceding çl.: He (the king) should levy taxes (kara) on the merchant, after considering with care the distance in buying and selling, the advantage gained thereby, the ex-

used. In IX 269 hanyāt if he can not catch them by spies, must also be understood as causal. So IX 276 definite penalties are given teshām chitvā nṛpo hastau tīkshṇaçūle niveçayet with distinctions between thieves. In VIII 34 the king ghātayet with elephants. In IX 237 the thief is branded with çvapada. Little thefts are to be punished (daṇḍayet) VIII 333 and theives are deprived of limbs, 334. The general principal running through these evidently points to the death penalty as the punishment in this earlier time and still retained to the law-book with an occasional modification.

penses (attending the trade), and the property (yogakshema or perhaps better the security) (of the merchant). Little by little should an annual tax be taken from the realm as the leech draws its food by little and little (129) (vāryokas is a water animal K. bee P.W. leech.). Exact regulations in regard to cattle, grain, flesh, perfume etc. follow. The right of raising the tax belongs to the king only on settled occasions X 128: The Kg. (Ksh.) commits no fault even if he take 25% tax on corn (though limited in the list just mentioned to one sixth, one eighth, or one twelth) *in time of need*, since he protects his people i. e. since the object in such āpat cases is simply that he may raise money wherewith to better protect the merchants etc.; from 119 this appears to allude only to war taxes (or Vaiçya can be well taken as a name of the whole people but) the tax can be raised on the third caste; the fourth caste, workmen, and artizans, must meet the emergency by work (120), thus denying a tax except by manual labour to these classes. K. adds more emphatically Na tu tebhya āpadi api karo grāhyaḥ. Cf. VII 137—138 The small dealers pay a yearly tax of no great amount — vyavahārena jīvantam (dāpayet). (K. those who live by selling vegetables, feathers etc.) (yat kiñcid api k. svalpam) but the handworkers, artizans, Çūdras, supporting themselves by their labour, shall work one (day) each month (in stead of a money tax). The oft repeated axiom (VII 144 and elsewhere) that the king's highest duty is the prajānām pālanam is also the root principle of this law of taxation. Cf. such expressions as: The king who draws a tax or revenue (bali, kara, çulka) without giving his people protection goes at once to hell VIII 307. The protection includes inward as well as outward foes, cf.: By restraining evil subjects kings are purified as if by giving great sacrifices to the dvija VIII 311. In view of this protection we find VIII 304 that the king is granted a sixth part of all the virtue of his realm — on the other hand (arakshataḥ) he incurs a sixth part of the wickedness of the people,[1]) so Y. I 334.

1) This idea of reward for protection is thrice repeated. Protection of people gives him a sixth of realm's virtue VIII 304. Protection of

Gentleness toward his people by the king is also inculcated in VIII 129—130. Where the king is enjoined to use first vāgdaṇḍa then dhigd° dhanad° and vadhad° according to necessity, but only where each preceding is insufficient may he advance to the more severe. In the last extremity he must use all four. Y. I 366 do. but dhigd° precedes vāgd°.

Between the Ksh. in general and the lower castes the relations are naturally not so important and occur not so often that one find them frequently touched upon in the law book. The contact of Ksh. and Vaiçya, with the different lives they lead, and the absence of a religious connection which bound the lower classer to the Br., the quasi line of demarcation which, aside from the separation of dvija and ekaja, seems to run between the two sets of caste, the Br. Ksh. on the one hand, and the Vaiç. Çūd. on the other, was sufficient to reduce the practical intercourse of Ksh. and Vaiç. to the smallest degree, and the mentions of such relations occur chiefly in finable acts from one party to the other. The antagonism of two bodies in the state, distinguishing the upper castes in general from the lower, is sometimes implied as for instance III 63—65. Through bad marriages neglect of ceremonies, not studying the Veda, and contempt of Br. kulāni akulatām yanti also by çilpa vyavahāra — moreover çūdrāpatyaiçca kevalaiḥ gobhir açvaiçca yānaiçce kṛshyā rājopasevayā (v. also 65). The family (of the Br.) comes here to disgrace through performance of that which properly belongs to the Vaiç. and Çūdra. The Ksh. occupation is however not among the list of these disgracing employments, so in VIII 102 (v. p. 9) and others of like bearing. The Ksh. and Vaiç. are however in the list of upapātaka grouped together and indeed with Çūd. as antagonistic to the majesty of the Br. XI 67, and in XI 88, where the expiation for one hatvā - - rājanyavaiçyau, when engaged in religious rites, is the same[1]), yet

Br. gives a sixth of Br.'s virtue XI 23, and in view of protection he receives half the treasure one finds VIII 39. This share of a sixth we find already in the Ath. Veda as appertaining to the king. A. V. III 29. 1. though here in the under world: yad rājāno vibhajanta ishṭāpurtasya shoḍaçaṃ yamasya. — Sixth also in M. VIII 33.

1) Acc. to Y. III 251—2 the penance is the same if the offender

in 127 for the killing (without restrictions) of Ksh. and Vaiç. the penance is respectively a fourth and an eighth as severe as for that of the death of the Br.; for the Çūd. the penalty is one sixteenth.

We have thus examined the position of the Br. as he is presented for himself, in relation to his fellows, and in his relations to the under castes, and again the position of Ksh. in the like relations. There remains only to the completion of the inspection of these castes the question what are the direct mutual relations between the Br. and Ksh. themselves. Previous to this however there remains unexamined the position of the two lowest castes, not in relation to the upper castes, but in relation to each other, and in regard to their absolute position. Little as an investigation of these castes, per se may contribute to our knowledge of the relations between the Br. and Ksh., it is nevertheless unavoidable for the complete exhibition of the relations of the four castes since the presentation of the connection between the upper castes can only be made certain when we see exactly what position the under castes take in and for themselves. In some cases this must touch directly or by implication on the upper castes — we endeavour then to show first the Vaiç.'s, and then the Çūd.'s position in this respect.

V. a. We find toward the end of the ninth book the rubric according to which the Vaiç. is to direct his life.

The Vaiç. after being installed as a member of the twice born castes (kṛtasaṃskārah) and marrying (also conditional to entrance in active life) should be always engaged in (vārttā) business, and the keeping of cattle.

For Prajāpati, after the creation, gave cattle to the Vaiç., while he gave men to the Br. and the king. Let the Vaiç. not have the wish «May I not keep cattle», nor must the cattle be kept by any other if he wishes to keep them. He should know the relative prices of pearls, gems, corals, metals, woven stuffs, perfumes, and essences. He should also be

has merely the intention of killing them (ghātārtham samāgataḥ) and the penalty is doubled if the one assaulted be a Br.

acquainted with seeds, and the good and bad quality of land, also he should understand measures and weights, the good and bad quality of wares (bhāṇḍānām), and the faults and defects of different districts, the gain and loss of salable wares, and the culture of cattle, the proper wages for servants, and the various languages of men (bhāshāçca vividhā nṛṇām), together with the means of preserving goods, sale and purchase. He should devote his best energies to a just acquisition of property and should give food to all creatures IX 326—333. The Vaiçya in this description is a merchant, a farmer, and a keeper of flocks. The languages mentioned in the text are of course, as K. remarks, the various dialects with which he must be acquainted for the purposes of trade. One of the great occupations of the vaiçya, money-lending, must be comprehended under the term vārttā (326). More distinct mention fails. It is possible that we may regard this comprehensive and unexact term as an indication of the fact that this branch is not yet so settled a means of livelihood, we have already seen that it is not regarded in the same light as the other Vaiç. employments. Not that it is not approved and enjoined by M. in general, but the contempt with which the usurer is elsewhere spoken of, and the fact that it must be understood here, seems to point to the fact that there was a different esteem felt even for simple money lending, as well as usurious lending, in opposition to the other sides of the Vaiç.'s life. Cf. Āp. 2. 5. 10. 7. Kshatriyavad vaiçyasya daṇḍayuddhavarjaṃ kṛshigorakshya vāṇijyādhikam, where no distinct mention of money-lending is made. The restrictions too in regard to the per-cent which the Vaiçya as usurer may receive, are given with exactness in VIII 140 flg. In 142 we are told that the money-lender may take two, three, four, or five in the hundred, for a month's interest, according to the castes (the lower for Br. and so on K.) K. adds nādhikam, moreover this is where no security is given (acc. to Y. II 37. Kull. and the evident opposition to çl. 140). It follows that the Çūdra as well as other castes was protected in his money dealings, cf. VIII 152—153. The regulations in regard to compound interest (cakravṛddhi) are not in favour of the usurer. The amount is restrained in 151. The regulations for bail and deposit and pledges in the eight book show an advanced mercantile activity, and the interesting list of tricks and petty cheating in which the Vaiçya should not engage, betrays a familiarity with most of the devices of that sort known at the present day.

The Vaiç. may live as a Çūd. provided he can not support himself by his own profession (as we have seen that the higher castes may also descend) X 98. K. adds he must give this method of life up as soon as he has escaped from his distress. So his relations with the Br. when unable to support himself. He may not be compelled to serve etc. Along with the Ksh. the Vaiç. is especially forbidden to take no part in the occupations peculiar to a Br. X 78. The false Vaiçyas i. e. the Br. who gain a livelihood by the life of a Vaiç. are regarded, as we have seen, in the light of Çūdras VIII 102.[1])

V b. Of Vaiç. and Çūd. together we find little mention. In V 140 we have the monthly purification of the Çūdra declared the same as the purification of the Vaiç. The Çūd. is limited by the epithet nyāyavartin (cf. Y. III 22 with M. V 83.) The çaucakalpa of the Vaiç. here mentioned is explained by K. as mṛtasūtakādau the purification for a death or birth. The king is directed VIII 418 to give especial pains in making the Vaiçya and the Çūdra perform their duties; «for if these two were to deviate from their occupations they would cause this whole universe (idañ jagat) to tremble». The Vaiç. the king should cause to perform vāṇijyam, kusīdam, kṛshi, and paçūnām rakshaṇam — the Çūd. dāsyam dvijanmanām VIII 410; here kusīdam is especially mentioned. In the reception of guests, although neither the Vaiçya nor the Ksh. are really guests of a Br., yet the difference between them in regard to their reception is marked, for the Ksh. is received at least with respect, and eats as he will after the Br., but the Vaiç. is pláced together with the Çūdra and eats with the servants (III 112 v. p. 57).

We have already touched upon this grouping of Vaiç.

1) This çl. has been quoted p. 7, 9, 23, 78 from other grounds.

and Çūdra together in one law by which the two lower casts are presented as one body opposed to the two upper ones. We see it farther in the law of slander and abuse, in which the Br. Ksh. are placed together and the Vaiç. Çūd. follow also together VIII 277 — where the same relative punishment is ordained between these two as between the two higher castes, namely that the Çūd. shall be fined the middle fine and the Vaiçya the first or, according to the sum, respectively 500 and 250 paṇas. Far more than this grouping, however, is another point in the same çloka, which separates in the most decided manner the Vaiçya from the privileges of the twice born — to be sure a negative privilege but as a matter of law none the less important. There is namely the clause in VIII 270 ekajātir dvijātīṃstu (tu, in opposition to samavarṇe in 269) vācā dāruṇayā kshipan jihvāyāḥ prāpnuyācchedam, but, in direct opposition or limitation of this, the present çloka adds the restriction «chedavarjam», which excludes the Vaiçya from the satisfaction which he as a dvija has a right to expect. If it is thought this satisfaction is here annulled on account of the offence being mutual, there is to answer that the punishment is not so great for mutual as for independent and one-sided abuse. Cf. çl. 276 where the Ksh. is fined 500 and the Br. 250, with çl. 267 where the Ksh. çatan daṇḍam arhati, and çl. 268 where the Br. pañcāçad daṇḍyaḥ.

In Yāj. we find II 206, 207, the fines lowered, and the slitting of the tongue not mentioned.[1])

VI. We pass here to the Çūdra himself and his stand in the state. Under the foregoing paragraphs we have seen the general relations which the Çūdra bears to the upper castes, and in the last paragraph, together with casual mention in preceding sections, his position in regard to the caste just above him.

The Çūdra is not necessarily the only servant. There are seven sorts of dāsāḥ (dāsayonayaḥ), one taken in battle, one serving for wages, one born in the house (i. e. son of

1) Another point in which the Çūd. and Vaiç. are grouped together is that of the form of marriage.

a servant) one given or bought, one inherited, and one daṇḍadāsa, VIII 415. The first of these and possibly the second may be as well from other castes as from the fourth, and the last may be either Ksh. or Vaiç., since we learn from IX 229 that only a vipra is excluded from those who are compelled to work off a debt by manual labour. Though these seem to be given as kinds of Çūdras from the connection, yet the fact that captives of any sort in battle were slaves, or belonged to those who captured them, and that the poor Vaiç. and Ksh. may do service for the Br. for the sake of earning a living, may include these under the list. The Br. cannot however *compel* these twice born to do dāsa service. In regard to the buying of human creatures compare X 86 p. 28 from which it appears to have been a regular trade, since it is mentioned with tila, cattle etc. as an article of commerce, cf. Gaut. VII 14.

Complete obedience to, and servitude of priests who know the Veda and of noble householders is the highest duty of the Çūdra, and brings him happiness; pure, and obedient to the upper castes, of gentle speech, and unselfish, he attains the bliss of a Br., and the highest station in life (in his next birth) IX 334—335. Should the Çūdra be in want of support (*Br*. çuçrūshayājivan Kull.) he should serve a Ksh. or even a wealthy Vaiç., but let him serve the priests for the sake of gaining heaven, and for the sake of support, for his whole duty is contained in the saying: jātabrāhmaṇaḥ (acc. to Kull. = jāto Brāhmaṇāçrito ayam, Pā. II. 1. 69. Vart. 8). — The best business of the Çūdra is the service of the Br., whatever else he does is without fruit (nishphala) X 121—123. The rule appears therefore to be not that the Çūdra should serve all the twice born, but his service, as far as it is worthy of reward, is confined to that of the Br., that of the other castes being only a resort in case of necessity. There is here to be noticed the api of 121 *even* a Vaiç., as if the Vaiç. were seldom the master of the Çūdra. In the same book X 99—100 we have the *dernier ressort* of the Çūdra, in case there is no one of the twice born castes who can take him as servant. «If the Çūdra is unable to perform service for any one of the twice born, he

6*

should live, on finding his wife and son are near starvation, by the arts of a workman — any acts, by the performance of which the twice born are shown obedience, these acts of a workman, and the different arts» — (çilpāni vividhāni). The Çudra may then like the other castes change his profession to that of an artizan or workman, which is usually the business of the mixed tribes (ex. gr. armourer etc.), and we even assume, in accord with the later rendering, that the general çilpāni included Vaiçya occupations, for a surprising latitude is presented us in the corresponding arrangement in Yāj. The Çūdra in this case (çuçrūshayā ajīvan) is directed vaṇig bhavet çilpairvā vividhair jīvet, although with the addition dvijātihitam ācaran (I 120), from which we must draw the remarkable conclusion that the Çūdra alone of all the four castes is allowed to ascend in rank in time of distress, and although still devoted to the interests of the twice born, he nevertheless assumes the position of the twice born. This we may almost credit in the explanation of M., and in Y. we can understand nothing else under the direct words vaṇigbhavet. This may be added to the cases showing the division of the Vaiç. Çūd. is not so strong as the general distinction between once- and twice-born would warrant our supposing. We are told, however, in X 96 that the low man (adhama) who lives by the mode of life of one of high rank (utkṛshṭakarmabhiḥ) is to be deprived of wealth and banished — restrictive to lobhāt, through covetousness, which is thus not applicable to āpat cases, but is a general law. The case we have considered, putradārātyayam prāptaḥ, denotes however the last extreme of misery. It is nevertheless surprising that it is permitted the Çūdra (even to save his life or support his family) to break through into the sacred round of profession devoted to the dvija. In addition to the law of general life, we are told, too, (X 97) that through performing the work of another (paradharmeṇa) (no distinction of upper or lower caste, but upper is implied from preceding) he falls from his position. His own duty, though performed with failures, is good — not the duty of another, though performed well.

The Çūd. appears at times to have attempted passing himself off as of higher rank. IX 224 one who gambles with dice or with living creatures, (cf. IX 223) and a Çūd. who pretends to be a dvija (dvijaliṅgin), the king should cause to be killed. In Y. the penalty is a fine (II 304) and the offence is confined to the Çūdra's living like a Br., not like any of the twice born as with M. K. with his usual inclination to protect the upper castes translates ghātayet in the first case with «he should cause the hand to be cut off« and in the second (hanyāt) with «he should kill». Cf. with this passage IV 200 he who being aliṅgī yet lives liṅgiveshena is said to receive the sin of the liṅginaḥ, and also IX 260, among the thorns infesting his government the anāryāḥ — āryaliṅginaḥ, though here not used in sensu concreto being attached to nigūḍhacāriṇaḥ.

The Çūdra must have none other than a wife of the same caste, and his sons must share all the property equally even if he have an hundred XI 157. K. na utkṛshṭā avakṛshṭā vā . . . jātāḥ, that is, the usual right of primogeniture is denied the Çūd. caste.

The Çūdra is excluded from the rites of the twice born, indirectly in II 103: He who does not properly repeat the sāvitrī is shut out like a Çūd. from every action (or rite) of the twice born (K. from right of hospitality etc. but karman is also a sacrificial act or rite). So he is excluded (II 16 and 26) from reading the Veda, and XI 63 teaching the Veda to a servant and receiving instruction in Veda from a servant (but v. P. W. sub voce) are reckoned among the upapātaka. We have seen however that the possibility of the Çūdra's being acquainted with the divine knowledge is not uncertain, and the Çūd. is mentioned even as giving sacrifice. The Çūd. can perform the household sacrifices without the mantras, for: Virtuous Çūd. who know what is their duty do not do wrong, but obtain praise if they follow the habits (vṛtti) of the good, with the exclusion of the mantras. X 127. Acc. to K. quoting Y. (I 121) this includes pañcayajñāḥ or the five house sacrifices. Y. says, let him not omit the five sacrifices with the namaskāra mantra — he should also rejoice at the çrāddha-kriyā.[1]) In V 139 the bodily purification of woman and Çūdra.

In spite of the fact, that as we saw under the head of Br. and under castes, the Çūd. is abjectly dependent on his master, and the fact that the Br. possesses all the Çūd.'s property, and that he can never escape from his slavery, the Çūd. is yet presented as owning property and disposing of it, (and possessing slaves himself) (?). In IX 179 we are told that the son of a Çūd. by a female slave, or a female belonging to a slave, may if permitted have a share of the property. From the text though çūdrasya is to be taken with putraḥ yet it seems that the dāsī or dāsadāsī belongs to Çūd. K. says by a slave taken in battle etc. referring to VIII 415. Y. II 133 is equally unclear — dāsadāsi must be female slave of a slave or daughter of a slave to support which we may again quote Y. I 121 (but as applicable to Çūd.!) where Çūd. (?) is enjoined to be bhṛtyabhartar upholder of servants. In Y. III 241 Çūdrapreshyam is mentioned as an upapātakam. The word may perhaps mean merely concubine.

The women belonging to the Çūd. are not less carefully guarded than those of the upper castes: caturṇām api varṇāṇām dārā rakshyatamāḥ sadā VIII 359, cf. IX 6. Imam . . sarvavarṇānām — dharmam uttamam — i. e. law of keeping the wife strictly guarded.

The vṛtti (here jivikā K.), support of the Çūd., should be proportioned to the wealth of his master, and again according to his own necessities, the size of his family etc., and with regard to his strength and ability X 124; and in 125 he receives the broken food and the old clothes, the

1) It seems to me, however, that this quotation from Y. may not appertain to Çūd. at all. There is no reason why the subject of hāpayet in Y. I 121, should not refer as in 113—115. 117. 123. and many other passages, to the indefinite dvija, not regarding the çl. as dependent on the foregoing. It is not easy to understand how acc. to Āçv. Gṛ. Sūt. I 24. 12 the Çūd. can be present at the madhuparka and not hear the mantras since they are to be repeated just before and after the direction is given: dakshiṇam (padam) agre Brāhmaṇāya prayacchet savyam Çūdrāya.

bad corn and old furniture of the house. K. remarks (in accord with IV 80) that the private slave can alone be given these, since the ordinary Çūd. may not receive the ucchishṭa etc. cf. M. II 56. According to Y. II 296 (unparalleled in M.!) it appears as if the ucchishṭa were an insult, not a favour, to slaves, as to men of higher castes, unless we understand injurious food under abhakshya.[1]) The restriction to personal slave is in Āpast. 1. 1. 3. 41 not directly stated — (ucchishṭam) antardhine vā çūdrasya paryavadadhyāt (Comm. ācāryadāsāya vā çūd. . . ityarthaḥ. In III 246: In the çrāddha, respt. the pitryaṃ karma, the broken pieces that have fallen on the ground belong to the company of servants, dāsavarga, who are not false and wicked.

Wealth should not be accumulated by a powerful (proleptic) Çūd.; for when he has acquired money he is injurious to Br. X 129 K. by non-performance of his servitude. The tax paid by Çūd. is one of work to be done one day monthly. The Çūdra has however property rights: Dātavyam sarvavarṇebhyo rājñā corair hṛtam dhanam VIII 40. Y. II 36. Interesting is a passage in Y. II 182, where one who is made a slave by force, and one who has been sold by robbers, one who has saved his master's life, one who has resigned his support, and even one who has bought his own freedom (bhaktatyāgāttan nishkrayād api) is declared to be free. There is no corresponding sentiment expressed in Manu. From this we must conclude that the çūdrasya nisargajam dāsyam of M. VIII 414 could, contrary to M.'s assertion, in a later time be given up, and indeed through the might of the Çūdra's property. In order to have accomplished this however he must have had opportunity to accumulate a substantial sum. In this same passage from Y. (çl. 183) we are told that a Br. no longer remaining in pravrajyā must be till death a slave of the king's.

The Çūdra, as we have seen, serves as witness in courts for his own caste and on failure of other witnesses for the higher castes also. Incapable of being witnesses in general

1) If we understand under this what *should* not be eaten then the Na Çūdre pātakam of X 126 (below) was already out of date.

are however a slave (adhyadhīna), dasyu, and antya. But if the proper witnesses fail, slaves and servants may serve in that capacity VIII 70. He may not explain law in court (v. next §).

The Çūdras are like unbelievers in their pernicious effect upon the land. The realm that has a vast number of Çūd., atheists, and no twice born, quickly goes to destruction in famine and sickness VIII 22.

The Çūdra is mentioned as in a possible case a king IV 61. (The Br.) should not live where the king is a Çūdra (Na çūdrarājye nivaset), nor in one inhabited by unjust people, nor filled with companies of heretics, nor in one over-run with outcasts. Since we know that in later periods something similar to this actually occurred, and a powerful dynasty raised itself to the sovereign power from the lowest position, it may not be impossible to conjecture that this mention of the Çūdra king refers to actual occurrences of similar facts in earlier times, and on a less pretentious scale. That kings other than those of Ksh. rank existed is seen from the express mention of the arājanyaprasūtiḥ (rājā) in IV 84.

The Çūdra is not bound by the strict laws of the other castes in regard to the fictitious impurities and smaller crimes. Na Çūdre pātakaṃ kiñcin na ca saṃskāram arhati, Na asya adhikāro dharme asti na dharmāt pratishedhanam X 126. As the text reads we would indeed be compelled to understand that the Çūdra is capable of no sin whatever. Yet I think K.'s remark justified that this çl. is only an amplification or illustrative repetition of the preceding one, wherein the Çūd.'s perquisites are mentioned («broken food etc.» v. above). K. says in the matter of eating laçuna (garlic, forbidden the twice born in V. 5 cf. 19), and such cases, there is no sin in the Çūd., but this does not pertain to such cases as murder of a Br. etc., since the law which forbids personal injury, lying, etc. (given in X 63) is valid for all castes; and farther, under dharmāt pratishedhanam, on account of his being a Çūd. he is not excluded from pākayajña or simple sacrifice (v. above p. 85).

Finally the Çūdra is even an object of veneration if he

succeed in reaching a very old age II 136—137. Wealth, relatives, age, actions, and knowledge, each more than the preceding, impart honour among the three (upper) castes. Who ever have the most of these, and lead a virtuous life, are worthy of respect, and even a Çūd. when he has entered the tenth (decade) i. e. is more than ninety years old. Cf. also the following çloka, where daçamīstha is also to be understood of the Çūd., and way is made for him on the street (v. below). So Y. II 116. The practical result however in the case of the Çūdra was naturally a more theoretical than practical one — beside the rarity of reaching such an age the necessary bandhu if not vidyā fail him under any circumstances.

Çūd. and Mleccha are cast together as representatives of the madhyamā tāmasī gatiḥ, produced by actions in a former life, XII 43.

VII. We now examine (a) the relations of the Br. and Ksh. with each other in general, then more particularly (b) of the king and Br., and finally (c) king with his ministers. (a) In addition to the relations included under § 1 and § 2 we note the following universal statutes concerning Br. and Ksh. The relation of intercourse II 135 as follows: The Br. ten years old, and the Ksh. (bhumipa) one hundred years old, let one understand to be as father and son, but the Br. is father of the two. That is Abhivādane. The greeting between the Br. child and the Ksh. is as if the young Br. were father of the Ksh. i. e. the same formula is used. The Br. is however father of both, we have to understand as second subject the snātaka who is to be greeted by the young Br. and old Ksh. alike as father. Cf. II 150 bālo'pi vipro vṛddhasya pitā bhavati — but the Br. is initiated at eight (II 36).

The Br. and Ksh. are mutually dependent on each other. IX 322 Na abrahmaṃ kshatram ṛdhnoti na akshatram brahma varddhate — but together (sampṛktam) flourish here and in the other world. K. adds as explanation, the Ksh. protect the Br. in their rites, and the Br. know the rites for the welfare of the Ksh. Cf. preceding 320—321. Were the Ksh. to grow too arrogant towards the

Br., the Br. would prove his subduer; for the Ksh. comes from the Br. (321); for since water from fire, the Ksh. from Br., and iron from rock, have respectively their origin, so in their progenitors (svāsu yonishu) their universal glory fades. That is the Ksh. can as little injure the Br. as fire, water, or iron, rock. These çlokas are added to a passage which I have already attempted to show belong to the later part of the work. To 320 cf. Mbhā. XII 2937. Perhaps these are to be reckoned in the judgement given the former verses, to 321 cf. Mbhā. V 482. XII 2010. The verses seem almost proverbial.

The Ksh. and Br. are mentioned as partaking of the sacrifices together in the olden times. After remarking that beasts and birds may be slaughtered by the Br. for the sake of sacrificing, and for the sake of support of the dependents, Manu adds: this is allowed «since Agastya did so long ago, for there have been sacrificial cakes (puroḍāçāḥ) of eatable beasts and birds, even in the old sacrifices (of the Ṛshis, K.) and in the sacrifices of the Br. and Ksh. (Brahmakshatrasaveshu) V 22. 23. This passage is interesting as showing the reference to a former custom, and particularly so because with no connection of context that would bring them together the Ksh. and Br. are nevertheless alone mentioned as making sacrifices, to the tacit exclusion of the Vaiçya. As we have seen, none of the other castes are regarded as guests, in the full sense of the word, in the house of the Br., but the Ksh. eats apart from the under castes and according to his pleasure (v. p. 57) III 111.

The man who is intent on his own good (bhūshṇu) should not esteem lightly a Ksh., a serpent, nor a very wise Br., even it they are (seem) of little importance, for each of these three could utterly consume the man who despises them, therefore let a wise man never despise these three. IV 135—136. Y. I 153 adds «nor himself» (ātman).

The Ksh. should never take the private possession of the Br., but if not able to get himself a living he may take from robbers (dasyu) and those who perform no sacrifices (as the Br., in 16) XI 18. K. understands an exception to the first clause and translates dasyunishkriyayoḥ «From Br. or Ksh. who do not follow the divine ordinances».

If a Br. kill unintentionally a Ksh. he should give (to the Br. [!] K.) a bull and 1000 cows or perform penance for Br. murder for three years (against twelve) XI 128—129. Y. gives general subject, pumān, and omits akāmataḥ III 266. For mutual insults the fines between Br. and Ksh. are respectively the lowest and the middle VIII 276. Acc. to K.'s explanation of 273 the Br. would pay 250 (paṇas) for insulting a Ksh. with the palliation of reciprocated abuse whereas he only pays 200 without such reason for mitigation of the fine.

The Br. in the rôle of purohita and the kshatriya (rājānaḥ kshatriyāçca) are both representatives of madh. rāj. gat. XII 46.

(b) It is in relation with the king that the Br.'s contact with the Ksh. caste is most clearly depicted. Here we meet the former not only as a religious but also as a judicial power, and may most conveniently regard them in their relation to the sovereign as a body, and then as a council, or whatever they are by virtue of their legislative powers.

The king should honour the Br. of noble descent, for this is an holy unperishable treasure of kings, neither thieves nor enemies remove it nor does it pass away, therefore this unperishable treasure should be preserved by the king among the Br. VII 82. 83. The treasure here spoken of is according to Kull., Y.'s corresponding çl. (I 314), and the context, the food and clothing and support granted the Br. by the king, cf. 79: «Let him give support and property to the vipras for duty's sake». So in XI 22 and 23: The king knowing the number of dependents and the household, and also inspecting the learning and morals (of a Br.) should give him fitting support, and after arranging his support he should likewise protect him; for the king obtains by virtue of his protection a sixth share of the Br.'s virtue. It is through the foolishness of the king that the Br. is oppressed by hunger (21). So VIII 395 The king should always honour (with gifts, reverence, and kindliness K.) a çrotriya and one who is ill or sad etc. But the Br. may not accept gifts of every sort, nor from every king without distinction. Circumspection is here demanded as in such intercourse with general members of low castes. X 113: The king may be asked for the base metals and property by the snātakas who are in distress (sīdadbhiḥ) and desire these things, but they should avoid (a king) who has no wish to give (but cf. 114). K. seems to understand pṛthivīpati of the Ksh. in general, and even one regardless of çāstra (laws), he adds that Medhātithi and Govinda explain tyāgam arhati as being out of place, perhaps because it repeats VIII 389. This is in āpat cases. In IV 87 Whoever receives gifts from a covetous man and one who is regardless of the laws of çāstra goes to twenty-one hells one after the other (88 to 90, names of hells). The same hells with trifling alterations are prepared in Yāj. III 221 flg. for those who rejoice in sin, do not repent, and perform no penance. Knowing this, Br. who are wise and declare the Veda, desiring happiness after death, do not take gifts from a king. Here we have absolute negation of the right, but in 84 just preceding we are told, as stated above, that the Br. should not accept gifts from a king not born in the rank of a Ksh.; for from such a king it is 10,000 times worse to accept gifts than it is from a sūnā — butcher (shop). In IV 33: He may when hungry seek property from the king (Y. I 130 gives no restrictions in regard to the king). In XI 4 we are told the king should bestow all kind of precious gems according to their worth upon the Br. who are Veda-wise, so dakshiṇā for the sacrifice. That the king should honour the Br. is an oft repeated maxim, the Br. are thereby generally especially mentioned as those who are wise and worthy as in IV 31. VII 38. Acc. to VIII 38 the king finding an old treasure formerly hid in the ground shall put half in the treasury and give the twice-born (Br.) half, cf. 39. The Br. has (37) however all such treasure troves.

The king is, together with the çrotriya, on coming to a yajñakarma to be honoured with the madhupāka, but not if the sacrifice be past. III 120. The king's fort must be well supplied with Br. VII 75 to 78 (purohita and ṛtvij.).

The king must not be harsh in his treatment of Br.

VIII 32. The king must be just to his kingdom, severe to his enemies, upright to his friends, and patient with the Br. (kshamānvitaḥ). K. moderates this to little crimes (kṛtālpārādheshu) cf. 80 same book. Nevertheless the priest is to be punished if he does wrong. VIII 335 The father, the ācārya, the friend, the mother, the wife, the son, the purohita are not to be left unpunished by the king, nor any one who neglects his duty.[1]) Y. I 357, it is interesting to note, reads arghya instead of express mention of ācārya and purohita.

The king must yield the honour of the way to the snātaka II 138. The right of way should be given to one in a carriage, to one more than ninety years old (v. above), to a sick man, to one carrying anything, to a snātaka, and to a king, of these the two last are the most to be honoured, and the snātaka more than the king. K. warns against translating rājā as of Ksh. in general on account of 135. We have seen that implicit obedience of the king towards the Br. is demanded in VII 88.

The Br. is presented as lying outside the pale of the courts in his right to take summary vengeance into his own hands; he can punish offenders himself, for, XI 31 flg.: The Veda-wise Br. should not have any thing related before the king, but let him chastise by his own power (svavīryeṇa) his injurers, his own power is mightier than the king's; therefore let the dvija repress his enemies by his own power — he may use the magic çruti of the Atharva without compunction since speech is the weapon of the Br.[2]) Let him kill his enemies with this; but in IV 153 he is directed to come to the king if he desires protection: īçvaram . . . *rakshārtham* (abhigacchet). The mention of the Atharva shows that the power attributed to this work was firmly believed in, but it is not in M. included as a part of the Veda. The exchange of castes is mentioned in VII 39—42. The vinaya or modest conduct which the king should ex-

1) The list of those whom one should not injure IV 162 is similar to this.

2) So XI 86 pavitraṃ vidushāṃ hi vāk.

hibit towards the Br. *vinayāt* prāptavān Brāhmaṇyañca eva gādhijaḥ (42) K. gādhiputro viçvamitraçca Ksh. san *tena eva dehena* Brāhmaṇyam — is the cause of this exaltation of the Ksh. caste, (also through obedience to çāstra and avoidance of forbidden things) kshatriyo api *durlabham* Brāhmaṇyam lebhe. Muir has traced this legend, which shows here the remembrance of an exchange between the castes of Br. and Ksh. An implied exchange in the epithet of veṇa vājarshi IX 67 cf. Muir I 266 flg.[1])

(c). The king's dependence on the Br. as ministers and advisers, is a maxim that when followed places in the hands of the Br. caste a certain share of political power. Just punishment we are told is impossible if the king be destitute of ministers. So (Daṇḍaḥ) asahāyena (rājñā) na çakyo nyāyato netum VII 30; but, 31, praṇetuṃ çakyate daṇḍaḥ susahāyena. The ministers are described in VII 54 Maulān, çāstravidaḥ, çūrān, labdhalakshān, kulodgatān, sacivān sapta ca ashṭau vā prakurvīta parīkshitān. They must be thus of an old stock, acquainted with the law, brave, and well tried[2]) and of good family. In VII 56 follow the affairs of state on which the king is to consult with his ministers: Let him always with these consider alike peace and war (sandhivigraha), the occasion, income, protection, and keeping secure that which he has obtained. K. to sthānam daṇḍakoshapurarāshṭrātmakam caturvidham cintayet, but P. W. eintretender Fall oder eingetretener Fall.

The opinion of these ministers the king should first receive individually from each, and then their united decision, — he should then do as he pleases (57). One of these serves as prime minister. To the best of these, a wise Br., let the king give his most important advice consisting of six points (those of 56). Placing his reliance upon this Br. he should execute all that is to be done and after having had conference with him he should undertake the business (58 and

1) Cf. also Muir on the relations of the priests to the other classes of Ind. Society in the Vedic age, Journ. Roy. Asiat. Soc. N. S. 2. 1866. p. 284—5.

2) P. W. but K. understands labdhalaksha of knowledge in military practices.

59). These ministers bear the name saciva. In VII 120 a devoted friendly saciva is to unwearedly examine the grāmyāṇi kāryāṇi which we have discussed before. He is called *anyaḥ* (sacivaḥ), must therefore be in contrast with the foregoing adhipati of garrisons, who should, on account of *anya*, be also called saciva i. e. saciva is a general term and not confined to the king's counsellers. In (60) other ministers are mentioned, anyān api prakurvīta amātyān; these are to be pure, sensible, with understanding in regard to acquiring wealth, and well examined. General supervisors of all deeds are mentioned in 61—62. (63) He must also appoint an ambassador (dūta) who is acquainted with all the çāstra, whose gesture and appearance are excellent, who is of pure nature, skillful, and of good family (cf. 66—68). There is nothing in the description of amātya nor dūta that would compel us to suppose these ministers are Br. Y. I 311 Mantriṇaḥ prakurvīta, prājñān, maulān, sthirān, çucīn, taiḥ sārdhañ cintayed rājyaṃ viprena atha tataḥ svayam. The vipra and mantrin are here opposed and indeed vipra comes after the mantrin. The care of the realm is a divided one, thus: Amātye daṇḍa āyatto, daṇḍe vainayikī kriyā, nṛpatau koçarāshṭre ca dūte sandhiviparyayau VII 65. Daṇḍa is here translated army by Kull. and the amātya is understood as senāpati. Thus the chief general is one of the ministers. The punishment (action enforcing proper conduct) is dependent on the army. The king has charge of the treasury and realm (in general) and the dūta of peace and war. If the vain. kriyā is dependent on daṇḍa this can only mean that the general military power preserves good order in the state; translating daṇḍa with punishment we must give it another sense than seems necessary in the first clause. It is to be observed that the king himself is, according to the list which explains his acquirements (v. p. 69 flg.), necessarily in a position that obliges him to be competent of managing all these affairs himself, so that by the restriction koçarāshṭre we must simply understand that the king acted as his own treasurer, and that in the particulars named in the text he appointed representatives, and these relieved him from the immediate performance of these duties, thus practically of everything excepting that of the chancellor of the exchequer.

The king meets his ministers in the morning, and is indeed not called upon, as a king generally is, by his ministers, but vice versā. The *king* rising early in the morning should *wait upon* the Br. who are versed in the three Vedas and wise (in nīti and çāstra K.), and remain by their order — teshāṃ çāsane VII 37. (K. çāsana as ājñā also *order*!) This is of bhṛtya v. 36. The bhṛtya are thus here Brahmans, their çāsana is probably their decision in regard to points of law. Other than in 61 and 62 appear the supervisors whom the king is to appoint in 81; adhyakshāṃ vividhāṃ kuryāt tatra tatra vipaçcitaḥ, te 'sya sarvāṇy aveksheran nṛṇāṃ kāryāṇi kurvatām, that is these supervisors, adhyaksha, are to serve as a committee for examining the manner in which the different parts of the governmental business is conducted. In 61—62 the dakshāḥ are merely experts who are placed at the head of different royal enterprises, the adhyakshāḥ would thus be set over these. Adhyaksha is equivalent to adhipati in 119, and in 189 he is mentioned (balādhyaksha) as a Ksh. along with senāpati. In Y. I 321 we have the adhyaksha as term for business overseer (as in M. VII 81); they must be expert, skillful, and pure, and are ministers of the treasury department (perhaps under the direction of the king, or possibly by this time the king's personal supervision in this department had lapsed and given place to officers who represented him as in other branches). We have already spoken of the sarvārthacintaka in every city and the fact of the king's bhṛtyāḥ in the capacity of governers being generally rascals.

When weary the king places the head minister (amātyamukhya) in his place (VII 141) and (226) when the king is well, he should perform all his duties personally, if ill (not himself — asvastha) he should consign the whole to the bhṛtyāḥ [1]) (K. yogyaçreshṭhāmatyeshu). Arising in the last watch of the night with ablutions performed, attentive, having performed the sacrifices, and honoured the Br., he

1) So of judicial cases VIII 9 v. below.

should visit the sabhā (145) (cf. above 37 also Br.). After he has dismissed the court he should consult with the mantrins, ascending the top of a hill, or in the interior of his palace, or in a wood where there are no observers, niḥçalāke (araṇye) 146—147. Again (151) in the middle of the day or middle of the night . . . let him with these (mantrins) consider his duty etc. After having deliberated on all this with the mantrins let the king, having exercised and bathed, in the middle of the day proceed to eat — 216.[1]) The amātya is mentioned without regard to office in VII 157, so also in IX 294.

From these notices of the ministers the conclusion to be drawn appears to be that the ministers were not all Br. That the seven or eight saciva were Br. is implied in VII 59, where the chief is spoken of as a Br. But that these were to consider peace and war, which must also include the idea of advice in case of war being actually present, would seem to render it plain that among them men of practical military knowledge must have existed (or in other words must be Ksh.) and so K. interprets one of the epithets applied to the saciva.[2]) The amātya seems to refer to Ksh. as well as Br. since he is not exclusively or even expressly spoken of as Br. The overseers, either as spies or headmen can belong as well to other castes as to the Br. The Dūta may certainly be a Ksh. since we are only told that he is to settle war and peace and must understand the art of counterfeiting and detecting the desires of the ambassadors (bhṛtyāḥ) and foreign king.

Mantriṇaḥ appears convertible with amātyāḥ, beside the passages already mentioned the latter is spoken of in the ninth book: whatever the amātyāḥ or prāḍvivākāḥ do otherwise than should be done that let the king himself do and cause them to be fined one thousand, IX 234. K. under-

1) In eating he makes use of poison charms 217. 218 and in 223 must be personally armed, çastrabhṛt. The most extreme case is taken against possible assassination.

2) Still in XII 100 we are told that the vedaçāstravid is worthy of saināpatyam etc., but later the ministers were dvija in general, cf. Coleb. Ess. II p. 518.

stands this of cases decided unjustly through bribery in the courts. From the connection with the prāḍvivāka who is certainly a Br. the amātya is apparently also so understood. The expression (in 226) the king must consign all his duties to his bhṛtyāḥ must include the whole of the king's duties even military, it seems therefore that the terms amātya and bhṛtya were general expressions for the king's ministers covering as well delegates from the military as from the Br. caste.[1]) These were evidently grouped together under the expression niyukta, concerning which general officers and overseers there is an interesting passage, IX 231—232, Which ever niyuktāḥ destroy that which ought to be done, of those engaged in any thing to be done, being cooked in the heat of wealth, these the king should deprive of property (K. understands of bribery at law) and those who make false edicts and those who cause injury to the people, also those who kill women children and Br. together with those who serve the people, the king shall kill. In this passage are several points worth remark. In the first place this is an universal law for the niyuktāḥ of the king (niyukta means simply commissioner — the same word as is used to designate him who is appointed to raise up a son from a widow etc.) and must include all the officers set by the king over a position civil or military. The king is to slay them if they issue false edicts (cf. Y. II 240 where the highest fine is substituted for death) or injure the people (or ministers acc. to K. = amātyānām bhedakāḥ — causers of dissensions among the ministers) or if they kill women, children or Br. This must according to the law which denies the king the right of slaying a Br. exclude the niyukta from the Br. caste. It would be necessary to separate the second çloka from the first; but the makers of false edicts, corrupters of people, and so forth, seem to require that those spoken of should be the same as the niyuktāḥ. It is further noteworthy that the slayer of a woman and of a B. are under any circumstances liable to the same punishment, for according to XI 55 and 67 the first was only an upapātakam while the second was a mahāpātakam. Under viṭsevinaḥ is understood by Kull. çatrusevinaḥ, followers of the king's enemies, but we can scarcely understand anything else than favourers of the people which may well be understood as referring to democratic tendencies repugnant to the power of the king. Again in IX 272 the rakshādhikṛtāḥ (also officers appointed by the king) if they offer no resistance in abhyāghāta, invasion, attacks, shall be treated like thieves i. e. killed.

That branch of the king's cabinet which constitutes his counsellors during proceedings in the law courts is without doubt wholly from the Br. caste. In the opening çlokas of the part treating of the law courts (VIII 1) we find the words: the king should enter the sabhā modestly, accompanied by Br. and advisers who are acquainted with the mantra (mantrajñair mantribhiçca eva). K. translates mantrins with amātyās and adds also the ca. Y. I 359 says he should view the cases with the sabhyāḥ and in II 1 «with wise Br.» There seems in M. a distinction made between the advisers (mantriṇaḥ) and the Br.: we may perhaps understand under the first the authorized judges and under the second the Br. who act as spectators and unauthorized but permitted advisers. Acc. to Vijñā. Mitāksh. the Br. who are mentioned in Y. II 2, as judges are to be held apart from those mentioned in 1. Çrūtyādhy° means the niyuktāḥ, authorized judges whom the king should follow — on the other hand the «Br.» of 1 are aniyukta in whose wrong advice or non-advice there is no fault.

The king if unable to perform the inspection of the law cases should delegate for that purpose a wise Br. VIII 8. 9. cf. Y. II 3 and M. VII 226 where the power of the king in general is delegated under these circumstances (v. above). This Br. should examine all that is to be done, with three sabhyāḥ. In whatever land three Veda-wise Br. are assembled and the wise adhikṛta of the king they call that the sabhā of Brahm. VIII 10. 11. The Br. who represents the king appears as the only judge in VIII 60 where the plaintiff is tried in the presence of the king's Brahman (Nṛpabrāhmaṇa). There must be at least three witnesses. So the judge in the similar cases discussed in VIII 79 and

VIII 181.[1]) In 186 the king is also to be understood generally and means the king through his officers.

The processes which have been tried and decided by means of a false witness are to be tried again (by the judge K.) VIII 117. Y. (II 305) says the king shall examine cases over again when they have been unjustly decided, and the judges, sabhyāḥ, together with the former winner of the case shall be fined double the sum won. Injustice in the decision of the courts is equally divided between the actual perpetrator, the witnesses, the judges, and the king VIII 18, but when one worthy of punishment (blame) is blamed then the whole fault comes on the perpetrator. The king alone however in VIII 128 is disgraced adaṇḍyān daṇḍayan daṇḍyān adaṇḍayan. So VIII 13 abruvan vibruvan vāpi naro bhavati kilvishī.

The king should not attempt to settle disputes (of law) which occur among the Br. (dvijāḥ) in the different āçramāḥ (K. explains this of disputes concerning the meaning of the çāstra) but giving them the honour due them let the king with the Br. teach them their duty after quieting them with conciliatory words (sāntvena) VIII 390—91.

A Br. who lives by his birth alone or one who is only in name a Br. may be an expositor of the law to the king, but never a Çūdra or his kingdom would sink like a cow in the mud VIII 20—21.[2])

It appears then that the king was to regularly (anvaham, daily, cf. Y. III 359) visit the courts, that he was either to decide the cases himself or in cases that were impossible substitute a Br. for that purpose. Only the Br. is here mentioned as his representative. His decision and that of the judges rested presumably upon a consultation with the Br. who accompanied him to court and also upon that of

1) Prāḍvivāka, cf. IX 234.

2) K. observes the order is to be graded on failure of Br., Ksh. on failure Ksh., Vaiç., and quotes Kātyāyana: Br. Ksh. Vaiç. are allowable but Çūd. is to be avoided. According to Colebrooke this was afterwards modified so that the Çūd. could give judgement which was binding in certain cases. Cf. Coleb. Ess. II p. 495—6.

the advisers or appointed Br. if they are to be in M., as we see them later, separated from the Br. as judges. The fact that the king and (Br.) judges bear the fault of an unjust decision seems also to show that the judges who accompany the king as his advisers are participators, that is the Br. share the responsibility and guilt. The actual office of the Br. in court was that of adviser; when the king was unable, a substitute was of course necessary, but otherwise the position was one of reference to the law. The Br. was the embodied law book. On a matter of doubt in regard to a quotation from an authoritative text he was the referee and the precedents of the court are dependent on his knowledge of law. M. himself regards the understanding of the vedic works (mantra) as the necessary knowledge for these counsellors. The body of law is represented as a system where neither king nor Br. can give arbitrary adjustment to judicial questions but must act in conformity with that already founded. No power of readjustment of a case at law or of nullifying the verdicts of the judge is ascribed the king except where they have been manifestly unjust, and dharma and ācāra, elsewhere so emphasized, are to be regarded as a fact governing judicial decisions in court not less detracting to the individual power of king than of Br. Indeed the Br. had only to declare what this was and on violation of this there were strict laws as well against the Br. and the king as against the ordinary witnesses in a trial, and for an offence against the right the king and Br. are both to be fined. The Varuṇa whom we have quoted as lord of punishment is more specifically described as rājñām daṇḍadharaḥ (IX 245). Even over kings he holds punishment.

Again, in the practical power of the Br. ministers in general there is really an influence that has little worth. Theoretically ministers and advisers of the king, holding the heads of government in their hand, the individual power may at times have overtopped its legitimate bounds, but when we consider that the Br. ministers were dependent upon the choice of the king for their political existence the position must have been secure only in ratio to the submissiveness of the Br. to the claims of the king. But the Br. are not even theoretically freed from liability on doing wrong and from a life position in the council there is no word.

The king could at his pleasure dismiss all his ministers and choose others, were his own plans not approved by the ministers; that these had any controlling influence upon the king outside of that derived from superstitious respect is as good as denied by the fact that the king on consultation with all his ministers then follows what pleases his own inclination (vidaddhyādhitam ātmanaḥ), which may be a selection from the views of the ministers or might be opposed to them all. The Br. has however in this relation no absolute power in the state.[1])

Résumé: The main points in the constitution of the three castes of the twice born, and the one caste of the once born are, as nearly as they can be abstractly regarded, these:

The Çūdra, once born, is to be regarded in two lights — the one as general representative of his caste, irrespective of his master, where he is the abject slave of the twice born, whose touch is unholy, in whose presence the Br. may not remain, contact with whom is as polluting as with the lowest wretches and outcasts — on the other hand, as the settled servant of one master in whose house he is perhaps born, where his position is by no means so ignoble, though the fact of his slavery and lowness can not be done away with. The personal contact with the Br. is here greatly eased of the strict abhorrence with which the dvija is bound in general to regard the Çūd. caste. As a servant his position is not in many respects different from the, indeed, not comfortable, because dependent and servile, yet still endurable, and not very severe position, of an American

1) The legal arrangements in Manu in regard to law courts show a marked variation in respect to the development of this institution. Many as are the laxities and omissions the laws were nevertheless codified with some care. Cf. the defective but careful attempt at codification under eighteen heads in VIII 3. 7. 8. These crop out again inconsequently to IX 250.

house-slave prior to 1860. It is true that the Çūdra has no mercy to expect on insulting his betters and torture and death may be the consequence, but so long as he retain a respectful demeanour toward the upper castes he is tolerably secure from danger. His master may give him advice and bestow on him such old furniture and goods as are no longer fitted for the Br. himself. He has his family, and his wife is as carefully guarded from freedom with other castes as the wives of the upper orders; his daughter or wife if wronged by the upper castes have the right of law and a heavy fine is visited upon the offender; his master has indeed the right of punishing him, but only as in the case of son and wife, for his own good. The striking is moreover limited in kind, and the fact that he may not be smitten upon the back shows that even he had an honourable part of the body.[1]) He may not study nor hear the Vedas recited but he may be present at the small family sacrifices and religious ceremonies and is indeed even praised for so doing. His legal privileges are few but his rights are granted him with the other castes, he has the right of demanding redress for an injury of personal character even from the Br. himself, he is held separate from the very lowest, the mixed castes, and should hold himself from their occupations till driven thereto by want. He represents his master in occasional business matters. As a matter of principle he can have himself no property, as all belongs to his master, but practically he is a householder and receives a support suited to his need, and has property returned him if it is stolen; he is enjoined not to acquire very much but evidently often managed to do so, and if his property in the eye of the law is dependent on the whim of the Br., it is at least in respect to other castes not regarded as a fiction. The rights of the Çūdra are generally on a graded scale in respect to the other castes and here no distinction is made between family-slave and general Çūdra.[2])

1) In the last two particulars he stood indeed upon a higher level than the Negro!

2) How for the legal arrangements of fines in personal injuries etc. contained in M. were regarded as matters of fact and had a prac-

Distinct mention of Çūdra as teacher when others fail and the possibility of his being a king show that he sometimes gained a position superior to the one he generally occupies.

Vaiçya: In no one of the four castes is so little said of caste relation as in the Vaiçya. The settlement of his duties toward the other castes is very simple and the peaceful nature of his profession gave probably little occasion for complication of his political relations. As a caste he seems, forming the boundary between the twice born and Çūdra, to be on several occasions more nearly coupled with the latter than with the members of the dvija orders. He must on certain occasions eat with Çūdrās, for offence from him he alone of the twice born is denied the satisfaction of seeing his enemy corporally punished — he is the only one who can live in āpat cases as a once born (this acc. to the natural grade of the castes) and the Çūdra assumes under same condition his arts and livelihood. His position is, however, in general marked by the holiness of his being twice born — he reads Veda, gives sacrifices etc. Money lending seems to be regarded as his lowest occupation and unjust usury is forbidden him. His rights as merchant, the laws governing his mercantile transactions, even the price of his wares, are all settled for him by the king. His connection with the Ksh. seems to be of slight nature, in the list of fines among the four castes for mutual insults there fails any possible mention of Vaiç.-Ksh. fines.

Kshatriya: The common Ksh.'s sole occupation with respect to the other castes is to protect them from enemies and preserve the internal peace of the kingdom. His importance is next to the Br. of learning and repute, and in case of fines and punishments he is servant of the common law like other citizens. Certain Ksh. acted as generals, were

tical working, and how far they were held as legal fiction resulting from a desire to adjust and systematize the relations of all four castes before the law with arithmetical exactness, can not be my purpose to determine. That Yāj. however as a rule follows the arrangement of Manu and settles such cases also acc. to higher or lower rank, so well by stated amounts as by general determination, shows the relative worth of these laws was as valid with him as with M.

raised to the position of ministers, and apparently acted in embassies, the choice of these favoured ones was dependent partly on family, and partly on soldier-like qualities and moral virtues. The gulma show a well regulated and orderly military system, as does the description of the various modes of marching and fighting. The daily drill seems to indicate a strict discipline of the army. The Ksh. is particularly forbidden sensual enjoyments, probably because most addicted to them. He may at times teach the holy law, he is at all times to study, and be careful in observing charity and ceremonial rites. If poor he subjects himself to the Br. who must support him. The great representative of the Ksh. whose power places him higher than his caste and in whom the whole glory of his caste is exhibited is the sovereign, rājan, mahīpati, īçvara, pṛthivīpati, pārthiva, nṛpati, narādhipa, narendra, nṛpa, kshatriya (κατ' ἐξοχήν). The king like the Br. is divine and human, as divinity he is part of all the gods, above mankind; as human he is a ruler, not so much, however, the ruler and monarch as the protector and guardian of his folk. In this position he is subservient to the land and to custom. He is not free from responsibility for wrong doing and can be fined. In his own caste he is however absolute monarch and acts as commander in chief in campaign, so well also in actual battle.

He delegates his power in the field but remains the sole authority in the fray, appearing merely to order his generals, and not to consult with them in camp. He must understand all that appertains to the welfare of the state. He is not made impure. He is not only king but reviewing and inspecting officer. As general sovereign he may not make laws contrary to those already established in caste and society. At an earlier time, and in Manu in partly restricted cases, the king embodies at once the judicial and executive power of the state. Nothing is said of the king's resignation from power except as preparative to his own death: if permanently unable to perform his office he should die as a warrior on the field of battle, if temporarily ill he delegates his ministers to attend to his command, but the Kg. as general monarch is the only governing power except in his obligatory deference to the established custom of the land, in which he is instructed by the Br.; but he is responsible to the courts, and is fined more heavily than his subject.

Brāhmaṇa: some of the most important facts which I think we are able to deduce from the view we have had of all the relations of the Br. may be formulated into the following results.

1. The Br. is, neither as individual nor as a caste, independent in his actions and mode of life. (a) The laws as they are laid down from antiquity, and the established practices of all the four castes are as binding upon him as upon other castes; in no sense is he here a free factor in the workings of the state. (b) The laws *of his own time* as far as they touch upon criminal matters render him as subservient as the other castes to the governmental courts of law [1]) and the penalties for violation of the state ordinances are, though often of different character, yet quite as severe as those laid upon the other castes, on the one hand through a necessarily inflicted penance, on the other through his liability to jus satisfactionis, with the exception of capital punishment. He is as subject to fines as other castes, though here there is a difference of degree.

2. The Br. is, if we interpret logically the text as it lies before us, included among those who are for certain crimes liable to corporal punishment, a point afterward denied by the law givers and commentators, among [later] contradictory regulations by Manu himself.

3. The Br. is by no means absolutely held to his own caste, specific injunctions imposed upon him to act as soldier in emergencies, and allusions to his active service as soldier, show that the practical side of the Ksh. life was not unknown to the Br., and no caste occupation except that of the Çūdra was absolutely denied him in āpat cases, and he seems at times even to have been not unacquainted with this.

4. The Br.'s honour and the high esteem granted him depends upon his position *first as man and secondly as Br.*

1) The permission to punish offenders himself is confined to incantations; he cannot punish them corporally.

not as Br. alone. It was more to be a worthy man and not a Br. than to be a Br. but not a worthy man.[1]) His whole glory as a Br. is hinged upon his conduct as a man, and the Br. is even recognized merely as a human being whose connection with other men must be of moral excellence and whose bearing toward them must be that of a friend — otherwise he does not rank as a Br. In no practical relation is the Br. who rests his claims of worth simply on his being of Br. origin (jātimātropajīvin) spoken of with respect[2]) but on the contrary often with contempt.

5. Inside the judicial power of the realm there was in the caste of the Br. a power that in certain cases could give arbitrary decisions on matters relating to their own caste and declare law where precedent failed — how far, however, and in what respects this judicial power could render decisions is not declared.

6. As member of the body politic the Br. has no part except as adviser, when he is elected to the post of minister of the king; there is however no legal power granted the Br. in this capacity, and members of other castes (perhaps however only Ksh.) share this honour with him. As judge in the courts he is a simple explainer of the law, and declares punishment according to the statutes already in force. He is the king's adviser, and in this particular the governing

1) It is no contradiction to this when we read that a Br. might slay all the worlds provided he repeated holy texts enough, or that the Br. is pure whatever he does — on the contrary, the very enormity of the crimes with which such universal absolution of the sinner is connected, prove that they are not regarded as serious facts; and when we read that the Br. possesses the whole universe and all that is on earth is his own property, but, again, that he must pay a fine if he rob a man of low caste; or that the Br. is as pure as fire, but again that he must purify himself if he touch certain objects; the conclusion naturally presents itself that we must regard the specific case with its practical consequence as giving the true light on the position of the Br. in such circumstances, and that the other statements are the utterances of a theory which, grounded on a theological conception, and favoured by priestly arrogance, never found force enough as a practical fact to affect the true relations which the Br. bore to the lower castes.

2) He may interpret law for instance, but only where better Br. are not to be had

power in adjusting legal questions but only as delivering the law, never as enacting general law, which power lies wholly with the king.

I close here this view of the Manavic caste system. The general relations of the castes speak for themselves through the juxtaposition in which I have endeavoured to arrange, according to order, all statements which are to be found in the Çāstram regarding the four bodies politic. The more important facts I have sought to bring forward in the final résumé. At the commencement of this paper I stated that the relations of the castes did not appear to have reached that last position which has been predicated of them. It was not my object to give a systematic exhibition of the modifications which seem to have first been introduced by the later law-book. These have been discussed however as they have at times come to view in the course of the treatment of the main question with which the paper is concerned. A thorough comparison of Manu with Yājñavalkya lies outside the purpose in hand; yet, though the presentation of the caste system in Manu, which we have here attempted, can properly only serve as a foundation for a critical comparison with the later work, and cannot be perfect till the complete arrangement of the caste relations is made plain (on the one hand grounded on the statements of Manu, on the other on those of Yājñavalkya) I may nevertheless be allowed to call attention to the following points gathered from the foregoing essay, in which an important factor in the caste system seems to have had rights more enlarged, liabilities less heavy, in the later work; in which the Br. is seen more highly seated above the other castes than in the law of Manu, and in which, therefore, we see the political organisation, not «in ganzer Vollendung» but still in a process of development; a process to be sure nearly completed, since the points yet failing are not of weighty importance, but which nevertheless has yet to find its perfection in the statutes of the later law. Notice the annexed differences: X 116 v. p. 9, sevā, not necessarily in āpat cases and without exclusion of Br. among the jīvanahetavaḥ — Y. limits to āpat. VIII 284 low penalty for personal injury, apparently regarding utkṛshṭa and apakṛshṭa but limited by Kull. to same caste and made indefinite by Yāj. through «nara» — v. p. 10. VIII 114. 115 general punishment and trial of witness, first limited in Yāj. to the Çūdra in all dangerous cases, while the trial in which no risk is run is alone given the Brahman. v. p. 11. VIII 177 where logically the Br. in debt with a Br. must work it off, though else enjoined to pay it by degrees — in Yāj. «equal caste» omitted, and «lower» retained. v. p. 13. VIII 268, Manu compels the Br., by stating an exact sum, to give satisfaction to the Çūdra on the former insulting him — in Yāj. the precise liability of the Br. toward the low class is modified by the law being stated only in general terms, which easily admits of an exclusion of the Çūd.'s right, v. p. 14. On p. 23 v. the result that the predication of godhead of Br. seems to be a later addition from the epic in its strongest expression, and is sustained in Manu by only one genuine quotation. IX 235, Branding, elsewhere included under the rule that the Br. must not be corporally punished, must here be logically inflicted upon all castes, Br. as well as lower. «Branding» in Yāj. rests on a false translation, v. p. 30. Gradual exclusion of the under caste by Yāj. from a privilege given without restrictions in Manu. Cf. VIII 339. Yāj. II 166. v. p. 52. Instruction (in Veda) received in time of distress from a low man, implies from context Çūdra as teacher (of adhyayanam), is limited by Kull. to all except Çūdra, and the case is not among the possibilities of āpat discussed by Yāj. II 241—242. v. p. 53. The expression «any one not a Br.» is modified by Kull. to Çūdra to rid the twice born of the imposed death penalty for inchastity. It can only (as shown p. 58. 59. on VIII 359) mean «all those not Br.»; Yāj. gives no such severe law. IX 224, a Çūdra pretending to be a Br. (or dvija) shall be killed; in Yāj. only a fine, but the offence is confined to Vipra, K.'s translation of ghātayet is «kill» only when applicable to Çūdra, in other uses of same passages he renders with «cut» v. p. 85. Among the list of those liable to be punished by the king Manu expressly mentions the purohita and the ācārya;

Yāj. substitutes the general «arghya» «one worthy of honour», for this express mention of the Brahman. VIII 335. v. p. 93. The simple mention of the thief and his punishment, already modified in the later discussion of the point by Manu, is by Yāj. and by Kull. exactly reversed in adjustment of the crime and the offended one, whereas the sinner is a Br. in Manu, and the gold stolen is not the property of any one expressly named, in Yāj. the sinned against is the Br. and the sinner is one of the lower castes, cf. VIII 314—316, XI 101. Yāj. III 257 and v. discussion on p. 73 flg.

The preservation of the Br. from the punishment enjoined in Manu is the cause of the altered circumstances in the later text.

These thirteen differences and modifications I deem a justification of the statement that the Br. has not yet reached in Manu that final supremacy which he afterwards enjoys, and a proof that the development of the political organisation has not yet attained its highest point. Lofty as was the superiority of the Manavic Brahman, his ambition was not yet satisfied, and his absolute ascendency was not yet complete. The Buddhistic reaction did not lessen the claims of the priesthood, but seems rather to have intensified them; and while the foundation of the long undisputed despotism was being undermined, the Brahman held the reins of power with a still tightening grasp, and strove, long after the completion of the Manavic law, to exalt himself yet higher above those whom superstition and ignorance and his own unconquerable pride had not yet reduced to the level demanded by his arrogance and his ambition.

Index of References to Mān.dh.çās.

XII.